THE TEACH YOURSELF BOOKS

EDITED BY LEONARD CUTTS

GARDENING

Uniform with this volume and in the same series

Prepared under the Editorial Direction of
Dr. S. Graham Brade-Birks
M.Sc.(Manc.), D.Sc.(London)

Farming

Good Control of Insect Pests

Good Farm Accounting

Good Farm Crops

Good Farming by Machine

Good Farm Workmanship

Good Fruit Farming

Good Soil

Good Grassland

Good and Healthy Animals

Good Market Gardening

Good Milk Farming

Good Pig Keeping

Good Poultry Keeping

Good Sheep Farming

TEACH YOURSELF

GARDENING

By

RICHARD SUDELL
F.R.H.S., F.I.L.A.

THE ENGLISH UNIVERSITIES PRESS LTD
102 NEWGATE STREET
LONDON, E.C.1

First printed 1943
Completely revised edition 1946
This impression 1960

Printed in Great Britain for the English Universities Press, Limited, by Richard Clay and Company, Ltd., Bungay, Suffolk

CONTENTS

LIST OF ILLUSTRATIONS

PLATES

Between pages 112–113

CHAPTER I

HOW TO BEGIN

IF you live in the country, you naturally acquire some knowledge about the cultivation of plants. It happens subconsciously, even though your main interests may be elsewhere. Most of us, however, are born in towns, and it is not surprising that the art of growing plants is little understood. I have worked for many years among town-dwellers in districts where no private gardens exist, except such as are made in window-boxes or on roofs. These makeshift gardens have impressed me much, for they are evidence of the innate desire of the average man and woman to practise the art of gardening.

Town-dwellers quickly learn. I remember taking a group of unemployed men (during the depression that followed the first Great War) from Southwark, in the heart of London, to Bromley. We acquired a few acres of land on which to cultivate allotments. All the men had been on the dole for months. They were skilled artisans, electricians, engineers, and so on. The Mayor of Southwark came with us, and cut the first sod, and we both spoke of the value to the individual, the neighbourhood and the State of home food production. Soon nearly a hundred men were finding a new freedom, and a new interest. They had to travel eight miles each way to reach their plots, and to obtain tools and seeds we had to form a small society. It was all hard work, but the scheme prospered, and by consultation with other gardeners, poring over books in the public libraries, and by experiment and experience, these men TAUGHT THEMSELVES GARDENING. They produced crops that

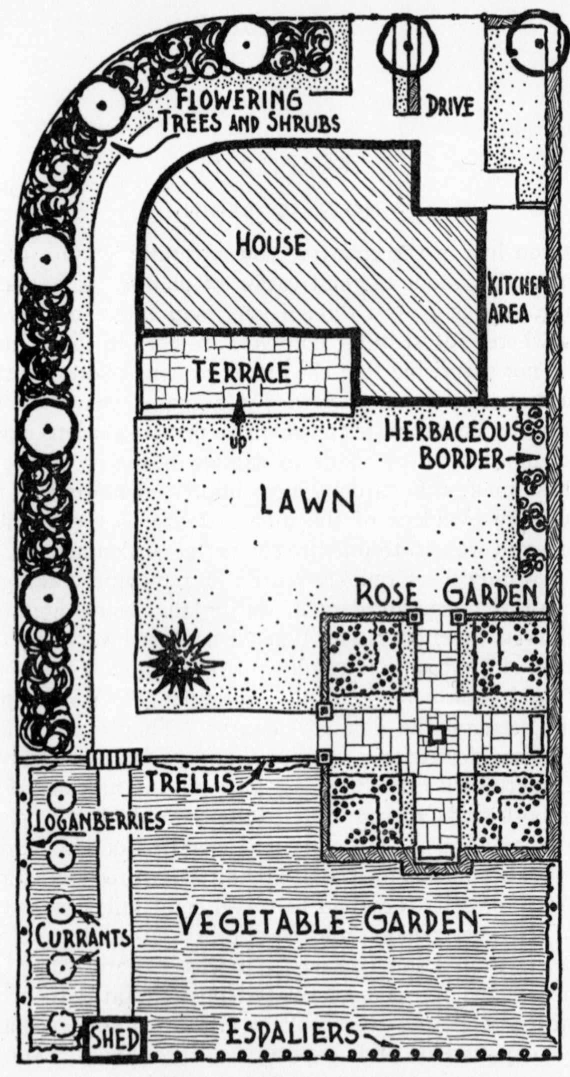

FIG. 1.—A simple layout.

Before you begin gardening on a bare plot, make a simple layout, as shown above, with areas allotted for your family's needs.

compared very favourably with those raised by gardeners of long experience.

Later, when trade revived, I had the pleasure of seeing many of those men move out from the congested borough of Southwark into areas where they had their own gardens, and where they have doubtless raised food for their families for many a year.

HOW PROFESSIONALS STARTED

"From little acorns . . ." Some of our most famous nurseries were started by men who taught themselves gardening. Carter's Tested Seeds, Raynes Park, owes its existence to the fact that a Mr. Carter, schoolmaster, brought back some aster seeds from the Continent, and grew them in his garden. People asked where he obtained his seed, and the ultimate result of that simple beginning is still to be seen.

Baker's, of Codsall, was started by an amateur gardener who struck geranium cuttings and sold them for sixpence each. He saw there was money in it, and the rest followed.

Everyone knows the more recent story of John Russell, who raised lupins on his allotment. After selecting and growing them for many years, he was finally induced to sell, and the firm who bought up the lupins and sold them as "Russell Lupins" netted a fortune.

Amateurs are still doing pioneer work. I asked Mr. William Lamb, a successful London amateur gardener, to tell me how he began to take up this hobby. He said, "Well, perhaps a German bomb on my house during the first Great War, while I was still in the trenches in France, had a deal to do with it. On my return after the war I went to live in a rural district, and was blessed with a large garden containing numerous fruit trees. Gardening was thrust on me, as it were.

"The local Flower Show came along, and I was induced to send in a vase of sweet peas. To my surprise, I won first prize in this special class. The following year happened to be the Jubilee year of the Horticultural Society, and a Commemoration Silver Cup was put up to be won by the amateur gaining the most points at the show. I was lucky enough to win this, and though my sideboard is crowded with more silver cups and trophies than it can reasonably hold, nothing has equalled the pride and satisfaction of winning my first cup. The first step to successful exhibiting is surely to *join the local Horticultural Society* and meet fellow-enthusiasts. It is really remarkable the tips one gleans from a chat with an old hand. After a few years with local shows, with increasing success, I made my initial efforts at London shows. Here competition was on a much higher standard, and very much keener. With *experience,* however, success followed success.

"To all amateurs I strongly advise the acquisition of a greenhouse. One of my glasshouses is filled every year with begonias and hanging baskets, making a floral picture of sheer delight; but my favourite flower, the border carnation, has a house all to itself, and my pen fails in the effort to describe the beauty of some hundreds of border carnations dancing in the sunlight.

"One never tires of a garden. With our English climate and its ever-changing moods, there is a continual fight against the elements, always a struggle against garden pests, but always the ultimate reward.

"Then, as life hurries on, and old friends pass one by one into the shadows, the garden-lover has a steadfast joy and solace in his garden, to continue with him until Time, with him, shall be no more."

I hope that many of my readers will pass, as did Mr. Lamb, from small to greater successes, and will find, as he has done, the joy and satisfaction of TEACHING THEMSELVES the art of gardening. The great thing, I feel, is not to be floored by reverses at the outset. Do a little quiet reading and observing, for, as in other arts, a good start is half the battle. Once the principles have been grasped, Nature will meet you half-way. I remember once asking Sir John Russell, the Director of Rothamsted Research Station, about the possibilities of a new type of fertiliser. His extremely sensible reply was, "Ask the plant about it." In other words, use practical experience as a true complement to theoretical knowledge such as can be found in gardening books, and learn by your results.

CHAPTER II

GARDENER'S TOOLS AND A SIMPLE TOOLSHED

If it is true that a bad workman always complains of his tools, it is equally true that bad tools make a complaining workman, and result in inferior work. This does not mean that every gardener needs to have every kind of tool in his toolshed. A great many of the so-called "indispensable" tools can, in fact, be dispensed with quite easily, particularly in a garden of limited size, where jobs are small and varied. For instance, long-handled shears are a great help in clipping thousands of feet of grass edging, but in a tiny town garden, where there are very few grass edges, the ordinary shears can be used quite well, and with so little waste time that it would be hardly worth while for two kinds of shears to be stocked.

A good rule for the gardener who is groping his way to the knowledge of experience, is to buy only those tools that he feels necessary at first, and add to them as he gains experience. A digging-fork and a good spade, a rake and a garden barrow will take him a long way on his first garden-making venture.

However, perhaps the first thing to consider is the provision of a toolshed, so fitted up that each tool can be given a place of its own, where it will be available for use on demand. This means that each tool must be on its own peg, or in its own place in a tool-rack, so that the gardener does not have to shift a dozen other tools and oddments in order to get at it.

THE TOOLSHED

The garden toolshed is generally, in the small garden, also the potting-shed, and it is the starting-point of all garden operations. It is wise, therefore, to give it due consideration when the house is designed, or when it is first taken over; for a well-planned toolshed and potting-shed make all the garden work easier. For a one-man garden-shed, the garden need not be robbed of too much space. A structure 6 ft. × 10 ft. ought to be sufficient,

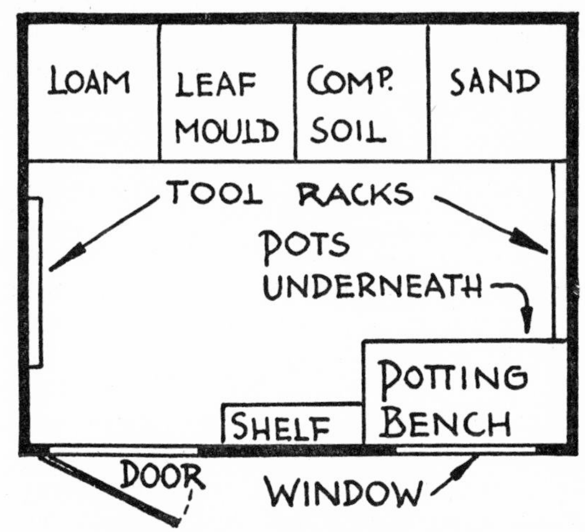

FIG. 2.—Plan of a simple garden-shed.

Showing the position of potting-bench, tool-racks, and bins for loam, sand, etc.

and an even smaller shed can be made to serve. The essentials for ease of work are these:—

1. Two racks for tools, one 6 ft. from the ground to hold the larger tools (suspended vertically), and one about 3 ft. from the ground to take the smaller tools, such as trowels, handforks and dibbers.

2. A shelf or small cupboard for catalogues and garden reference books.

3. A shelf or part of the same cupboard for tools,

such as syringes, that cannot be stored on the racks.

4. A cupboard or set of small drawers to take seeds.

5. A potting-bench. This, if possible, should be immediately under a good window. In height it should be about 3 ft. from the ground—*i.e.*, rather higher than an ordinary table. The exact height will vary according to the height of the user, but it makes for ease and comfort if back-bending is avoided.

Space under the potting-bench is useful for such things as flower-pots and soil. If the shed is large enough, a row of bins, open on one side, is a convenient arrangement for storing potting materials such as loam, sand, leafmould and peat. Bins are also useful for fertilisers, but these can be stored dry in their own sacks or bags for short periods. If storage space is limited, a good general fertiliser that will keep without deteriorating or becoming caked (see Chapter V) is the best thing to have in stock.

Insecticides and weed-killers, which are poisonous, should only be stored on a high shelf, or preferably in a locked cupboard: it cannot be too much stressed that the responsibility for these materials is the gardener's, and everything which can be considered dangerous, such as nicotine insecticide or arsenical weed-killer, should be kept under lock and key, and the key should *not* be left hanging in the shed!

As a last suggestion for maintaining the general tidiness of the shed, remember that there is always some waste material during potting operations—ends of raffia, broken stakes, worn-out soil, etc. Keep a bin specially for these, and there will not be a constant muddle to be cleaned up after each operation.

ESSENTIAL TOOLS

The essential tools in a garden vary, as already suggested, according to the type of garden and its size. The following comments concerning the various tools may prove a guide to the buyer, and the most essential tools are therefore described first.

Spade. "When Adam delved and Eve span" no doubt Adam used a spade, and so buried in antiquity is the origin of the first spade that we may well wonder if it differed at all from that in use now. Attempts are often made to improve on the pattern of the regulation spade—curved sides, pointed ends, etc. The ordinary D-handled spade, with a stout handle, and (preferably) stainless blade, is about the best thing that can be bought in this line. If stainless steel is too highly priced, the spade blade should be stout enough to be quite unbendable. A No. 2 size is generally suitable for a beginner.

Forks. Forks are made in great variety. The most suitable for general use is a four-pronged digging-fork, No. 2 size. There are also larger forks, and flat-tined forks that are suitable for digging potatoes and for forking over light soil, and there are much lighter "ladies'" forks, suitable for loosening soil among growing plants.

Hoes. The swan-neck, or Canterbury hoe, is the type favoured by many gardeners, and this is certainly most useful for hoeing on heavy ground and for chopping off stubborn weeds. The Dutch hoe, which is used with a push action instead of a downward, chopping motion, is very good on light soils. There are also modern types that include the advantages of both Canterbury and Dutch hoes. One is the Universal, a hoe the blade of which is sharpened on both sides, so that it can be used as a push hoe or a draw hoe, or pushed backwards and forwards through the top inch or two of soil. In another type a steel wire replaces the blade, and this is a very light and convenient tool for hoeing light, sandy soil. A triangle hoe is particularly suitable for drawing drills in preparation for seed-sowing.

Rakes. A steel, 12-inch garden rake is necessary to prepare and level ground. A wooden hay-rake is better for raking up mown grass, leaves and other light litter.

A stout handle, unbendable teeth and sufficient length to the handle are the points to look for in a rake. In addition, care should be taken that the handle and rake are securely joined, as there is considerable strain on this part when the rake is in use.

Wheelbarrow. An oak wheelbarrow, for wheeling manure, moving plants, etc., is the gardener's friend. There are also serviceable wheelbarrows in metal, with rubber tyres, which are easy to use, and generally preferred by women gardeners, on account of their light weight. If these are used, they should be regularly painted, or they quickly become rusted through and useless.

Lawn Mower. For gardens where up to a quarter of an acre of lawn-grass has to be cut, an ordinary hand-mower is good enough. These vary in size and in quality: some mowers are quite unsuitable for use over rough grass, and the advice of the salesman should be sought when making any purchases.

A quarter of an acre or more of lawn-grass makes the purchase of a motor mower almost imperative, for it does not pay to employ a man to cut such large areas with a hand-mower.

Garden Roller. A 2½-cwt. garden roller is the size generally used in the average family garden. It is not wise to buy a heavier make unless two rollers can be stocked, as the heavier rollers have a limited use.

Mattock. A Devon two-billed mattock is a tool

rather like two heavy, sharp hoes joined together, one on each side of the handle, so that by a twist of the handle one can use either the wide blade or the narrow one. This is an excellent tool for use where tree-roots have to be grubbed out.

FIG. 3.—Simple tool-rack for storing tools after use. The gardener's motto should be: "A place for everything and everything in its place."

Dibber. An improvised dibber can be made for a small garden from the handle of an old D-handled spade. It should be cut off about a foot in length from the top, and the lower end should be sharpened to a point. Smaller dibbers can be cut from pieces of ash, while dibbers for use among tiny seedlings are simply short, pointed sticks. A dibber is merely a tool that will conveniently make a series of holes in the ground surface suitable for the reception of seedlings, potato tubers, etc.

Sieves. A wooden-rimmed garden sieve, with ½-inch holes, diameter of sieve about 16 inches, is about the most useful tool for general purposes—that is, for sifting leaf-mould, potting-soil, etc. A piece of metal gauze fixed over a small, square frame is quite good for sifting fine soil over newly sown seeds.

Trowel. For planting seedlings and bedding-plants a trowel is used. Stainless-steel trowels are obtainable, and are a pleasure to use. They have 5-inch blades for general purposes, but for fern-lifting and planting, rockery work, etc., narrower blades are made. A blunt handle on the trowel allows for its use in firming the soil of pots and round newly planted seedlings.

Handfork. A small handfork, companion to the trowel, is a useful tool for loosening soil between seedlings, and for planting and lifting. The handfork with a long handle is generally called a weeding-fork, but can also be used for planting and cultivating.

Both these are also obtainable in stainless steel.

Bagging-hook. In a large garden, where hedge-bottoms have to be cleared, coarse grass cut down, and weedy corners cleared, a bagging-hook is needed. This is a curved blade, which must be kept sharp as it is used, by constant touching up on a scythe stone—a stone specially made for the purpose.

Shears. Two types of shears are commonly used in the small garden. Short-handled shears are used to clip hedges, trim awkward parts of the lawn and grass edges, etc. Long-handled shears are specially made to trim the edges of lawns without back-bending. There are other shears useful for special purposes, but they should only be purchased as the need for them arises.

Knives. The professional gardener does a great deal

FIG. 4.—Garden tools in wood and stainless steel. Flower baskets in wicker and Sussex trug. Enamelled metal watering cans.

of garden work with his knife. A strong pruning-knife with a curved blade is most useful. A smaller pocket-knife is needed for making cuttings, and, for budding, special knives are sold that have a blunt bone handle for use in inserting the bud into the stock.

Secateurs. Where pruning of roses, fruit-trees and

flowering shrubs is to be done, a pair of secateurs is essential. These secateurs make a clean cut without bruising the wood, and are specially recommended for use by the novice as well as by the experienced gardener.

Shovel. The shovel—a type of spade with a rounded blade so that it holds sand and soil easily—is a very useful tool. It is lighter in weight than the digging-spade, and therefore less tiring to use when quantities of soil have to be shifted. No. 2 is a convenient size.

Cultivator. To work between rows of growing crops, a three-pronged cultivator with a 4-foot handle can be recommended. It is easy to manipulate, and its use greatly improves the fertility of the soil.

Water-can. A 2-gallon water-can, with rose-screw for distributing water over seedlings, is essential. For greenhouse work a Haws-type can, with rose above the can spout, set horizontally, is best. A hose is a luxury which must in many cases be dispensed with, but hoeing and cultivation generally help to retain soil moisture.

Garden Basket. The Sussex trug-basket is handy for gathering crops, and for many other garden tasks. It is obtainable in various sizes. No. 4 size holds about 3 gallons.

Garden Saw. A small pruning-saw becomes necessary where orchard fruits are grown, or where forest trees have to be pruned in their early years.

Garden Hammer. A No. 2 garden hammer is a tool that has a variety of uses in a garden, and can be considered a good investment.

Gloves. Gardening gloves of thick leather are needed when dealing with roses, gooseberries and prickly shrubs. They are also a help in many other tasks.

Garden Pick. A 3-lb. garden pick is the tool for making paths, trenching hard ground, and opening holes for large trees.

Pliers. Pliers with a wire cut are desirable where wire is used for wall-training, espaliers, wire fencing, etc.

Garden Reel and Line. This is wanted for drawing straight drills and planting out seedlings in straight lines, but it is by no means essential that this should be a specially made affair. A stout piece of stick a foot long, pointed at one end, on to which is wound a good length of strong twine, is sufficient. The other end of the twine should be fastened to a second pointed stick. Both sticks can then be pushed into the ground where desired, with the string unwound between them just sufficiently for it to be stretched taut.

Garden Syringe. Spraying insecticides is an operation that every garden owner must perform, and in the little garden this is done with a hand syringe. The type that has a bent end, allowing for its use on the undersides of leaves, is desirable.

Edging Iron. To cut lawn edges where beds are made in the grass, an edging iron—a sort of spade with a half-moon blade—is used.

Turf-lifter. A special tool that allows turf to be lifted in pieces suitable for re-laying is called a turf-lifter, and is an essential for new garden layouts where these are on a large scale. Other, and less essential but sometimes desirable tools are listed in trade catalogues. In addition, a stock of garden labels, a garden pencil, a hatchet for sharpening stakes, an outdoor thermometer with maximum and minimum reading, a greenhouse thermometer (if a glasshouse is in the garden), a supply of tying materials, including raffia, soft string and tarred twine, are oddments that the gardener must consider. Then, of course, there are such special tools as a collection of rock-garden tools in a small kit, for the rockery specialist. These out-of-the-ordinary tools will be added as the need arises.

GENERAL CARE OF THE TOOLS

Care of garden tools is very important: they last many times as long if they are properly looked after all the time.

All stainless-metal tools should be washed after use and then put away in their place. Tools of other metal should be cleaned and then rubbed with an oily rag before they are put away.

Wooden-handled tools must never be left out in rain or during damp nights, but must be stored in the dry shed; otherwise the wood eventually decays and the tool becomes useless.

It adds to the gardener's ease in collecting up tools after use, if the smaller tools are painted some bright colour. A bright delphinium blue or geranium red on the handle of the trowel and handfork makes them conspicuous from some distance, and there is less likelihood of their being left outdoors.

All cutting tools, including hoes and spades, should be kept sharp enough to do their work efficiently.

CHAPTER III

WHY WE NEED A PLAN IN GARDEN-MAKING

UNLESS you have a clear idea of what you mean to do with a garden, you are likely to have difficulties, and still more likely to find you have wasted your labour; so a garden plan may be regarded as essential, whatever the size of the plot.

The method of making the plan is this: First measure the boundaries of the plot. The use of squared paper is helpful: each square will be equivalent to a certain plot measurement—say, to 10 feet each way. If you

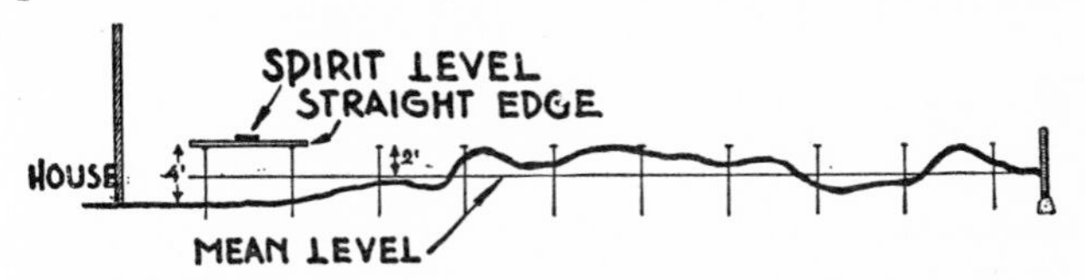

FIG. 5.—Simple method of levelling a piece of ground.

A straight-edge and spirit-level are used from peg to peg. This method is suitable for small areas : for larger areas, boning-rods or dumpy level are necessary.

transfer all the straight boundary lines to the paper, keeping to this scale, you will find it comparatively easy to plan your various features without making serious mistakes.

Note views from the garden, if any, that you would like to keep. Note shrubs and trees: on no account move these or destroy them until you have quite finished your plan, for you may find them helpful in picture-making. Then note levels. Boning-rods will be of great assistance in this connection. These are 3-foot rods, each with a 1-foot piece of wood across the top, forming a T. Begin at one end—say the back door of a small house—and with the help of friends, take " sights " from the first rod, across the second, to the third. In this way you will be able to see accurately where the rise and fall of the ground-surface occurs, and how much fall there is. You can calculate how much soil or rock will have to be removed if you wish to make the ground quite level.

In a small garden you will be able to manage these measurements and their translation to the squared paper quite well, but in a very large garden it is worth while to make more exact measurements, and what is known as a

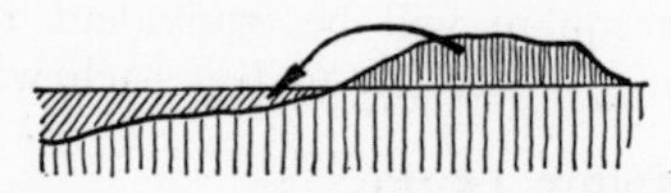

FIG. 6.—The " cut-and-fill " method of levelling. A mean level is obtained to avoid much labour.

Surveyor's " dumpy level " is used. With this instrument used approximately in the middle of the plot, all the levels can be worked out. You can arrange for the loan of the instrument by a local builder, or, preferably, in a large garden, you would be wise to have the ground surveyed for a small fee.

Planning is a vast and interesting subject, and one that in itself fills many volumes on the gardener's bookshelf. Obviously it cannot be properly dealt with here, but the following brief summary of suggestions will prove a useful basis for the man who wishes to plan his own garden on common-sense lines, and without making too many mistakes.

1. First make a list of the special needs of the household. A growing family may need a children's

corner and a vegetable garden, or a games section. Older people may want rest and privacy. Note that a garden can be laid out to grow with the changing needs of a family—a children's corner designed to become ultimately a water garden or rose garden, for instance.

2. Next write down *in order of personal preference* the features you will consider for inclusion in the design—lawns, herbaceous borders, formal beds, sunk gardens, alpine or rock gardens, special flower garden (rose, iris, carnation, heather, etc.), vegetable garden, fruit orchard, herb garden, shrubberies, pergolas, paved gardens and walks, and so on.

3. Consider what sheds and glasshouses can be erected.

4. Consider what paid and unpaid labour can be spent on garden maintenance, after the initial layout is complete. (This may make some difference to the order of preference in which you list the main features !)

At this stage make a very rough drawing of your garden outlines, boundaries, etc., and try to fit into these the various sections on which you have set your heart. Remember to choose sites that will suit. The rock garden, for instance, should be in full sun: if you plan it in the shade it will have to be planted mainly with ferns, and will not be a colourful rock garden that is a blaze of beauty in early summer. A water garden should be in the lowest part of the grounds. Fruit is best if grown on a plot sheltered from the east. Vegetables require an open, sunny site.

As you roughly indicate these on your paper, remember the position of house windows, doors and entrance paths:

each should have its planned picture. To open a garden door and see nothing at first but a concrete path and evergreen hedge is not encouraging.

Above all, remember that every garden feature has to be serviced: good paths should make all parts of the garden accessible with the barrow, so that gardening is easy in all weathers. Service paths must also allow a visitor to stroll through the garden, from feature to feature, without being forced to return always by the same path.

Finally keep in mind the use of the garden as a part of the house: seats in sheltered corners, and some shade where it is likely to be appreciated should generally be priority features.

It is interesting to plan a garden in this way, but it will not be found easy by those who know little of gardening. All sorts of difficulties arise: you want to put the greenhouse near the garage, but that part of the garden is too shady; or you have a group of silver birches just where you would have made a rose garden, and of course, well-grown trees cannot be moved. A dozen and one other problems have to be solved on each special garden plan; that is why one cannot adopt blindly any ready-made plan, but it is also what makes garden planning so interesting. It satisfies as a hobby because it is essentially creative.

The best advice I can give to any gardener who plans a new garden is that he should borrow as many books as he can on the subject of Landscape Architecture, and study them all before he makes his mind up finally on the style of garden he wants.

SPECIMEN PLANS

Now a word about the plans which are reproduced here as specimens. They are plans prepared for actual garden sites, with the difficulties and opportunities that each site presented—sloping ground, existing banks of

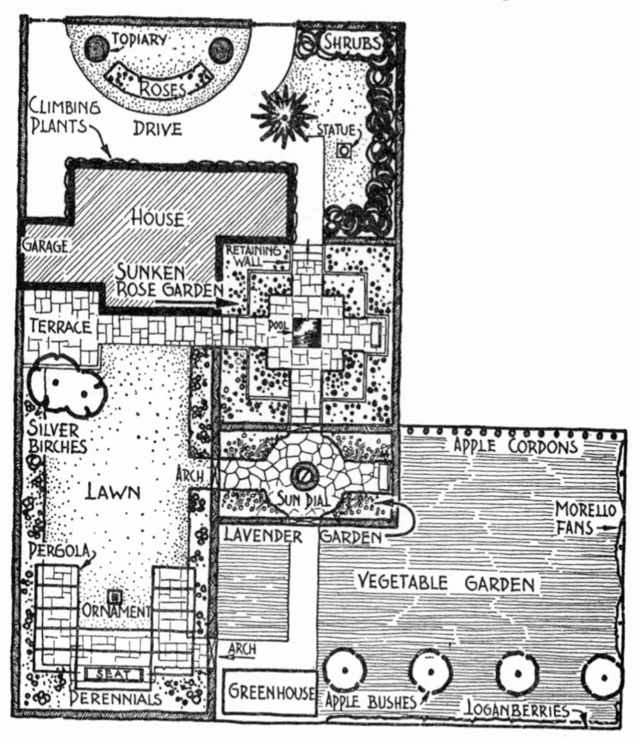

FIG. 7.—Plan of a small garden.
Showing division into areas for food production and recreation. Fruit is planted against fences to economise space.

trees and so on. *Your* site may have some of these features, or it may be a flat square or oblong site with no particular character when you take it over. In any case the new garden is to be yours, but it may help if you study each of these plans and try to discover why each has been developed as you see it here.

You can "lift" a bit from one plan, and a bit from another. You can transpose parts. You can simplify or amplify. But whenever you plan an alteration,

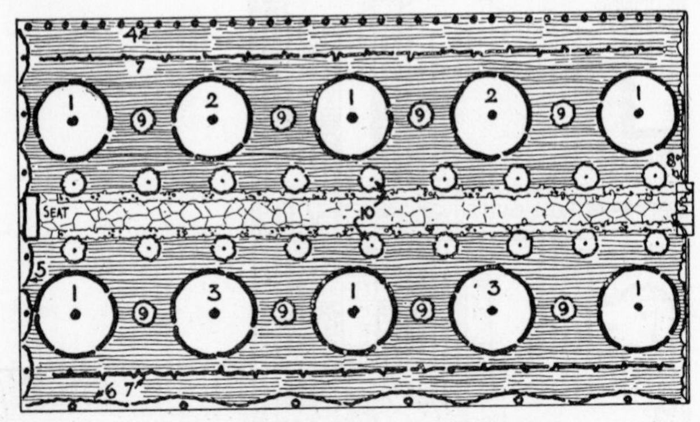

Fig. 8.—Simple plan of a fruit garden.

1. Apple (bush).
2. Pear ,,
3. Plum ,,
4. Apple, cordons.
5. Pear, espaliers.
6. Morello, fans (north side).
7. Raspberries.
8. Loganberries on trellis and arch.
9. Gooseberries.
10. Black and red currants.

Crazy paved path, edged by aubrietias, arabis and similar cushion-like perennials.

think well all round the subject first. If you decide to move a section such as the fruit patch, and put it in another part of the plot, ask yourself whether this will expose the fruits to cold winds or eastern—early morning—frosts, which are particularly troublesome among fruits.

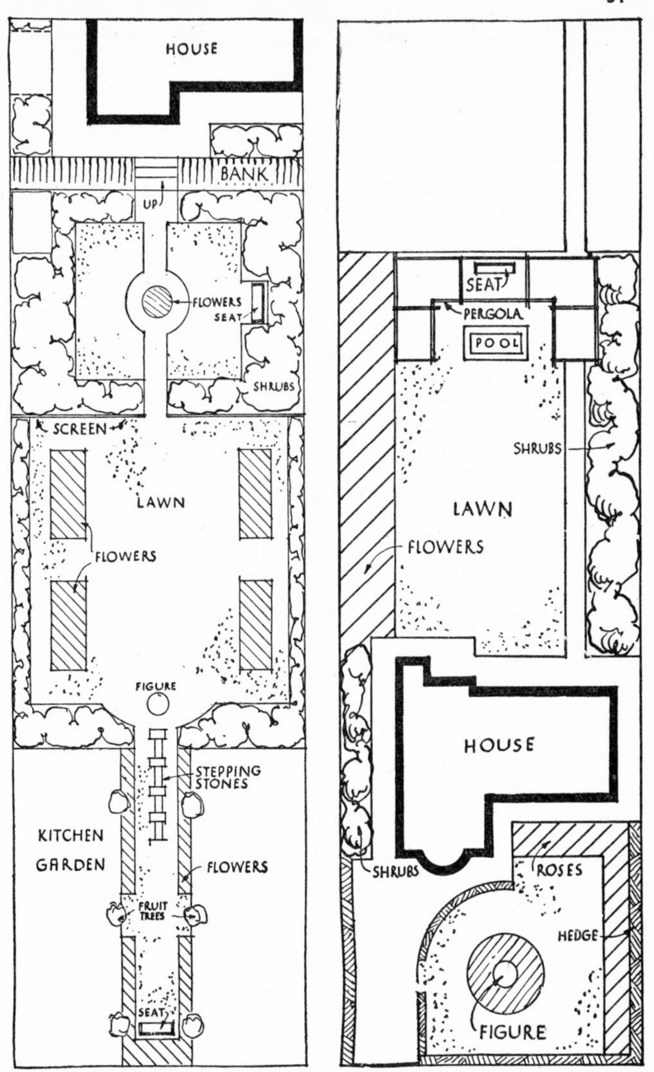

FIG. 9.—Note: vegetable garden is placed at the ends.

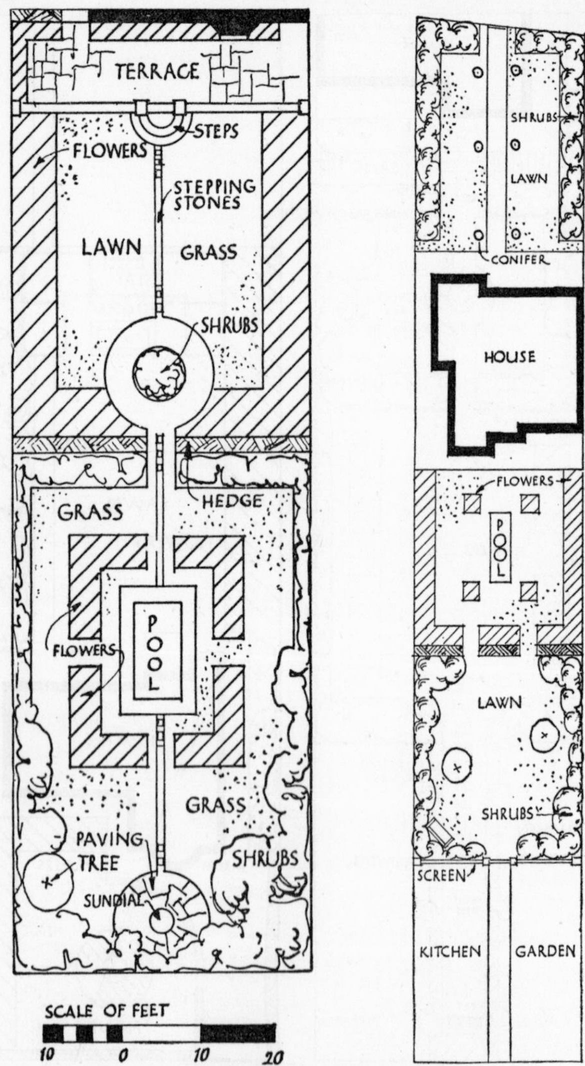

FIG. 10.—Formal flower gardens with lily pools.

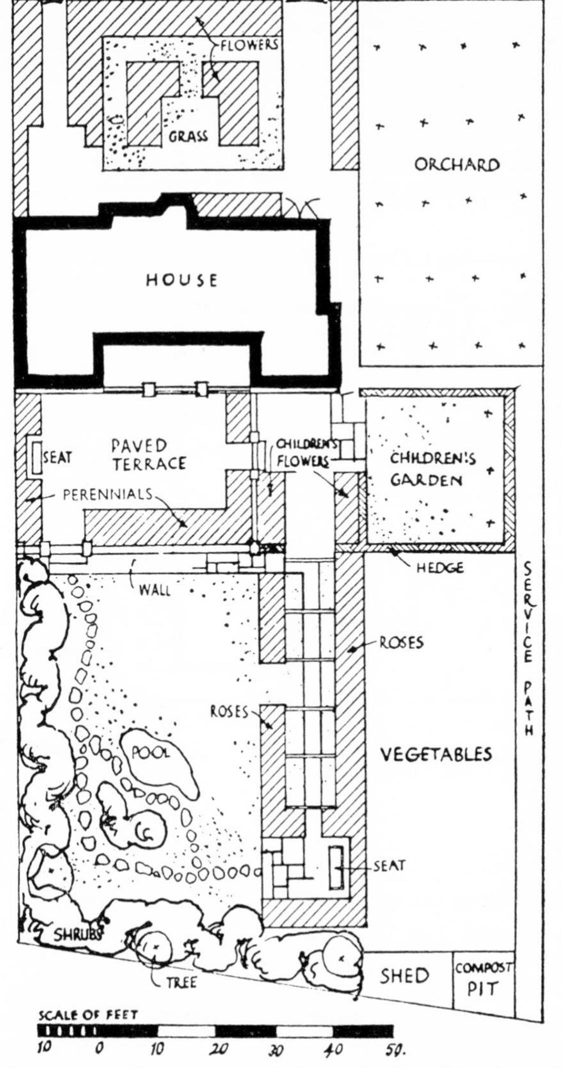

FIG. 11.—A side plot is used for orchard, children's garden and vegetables.

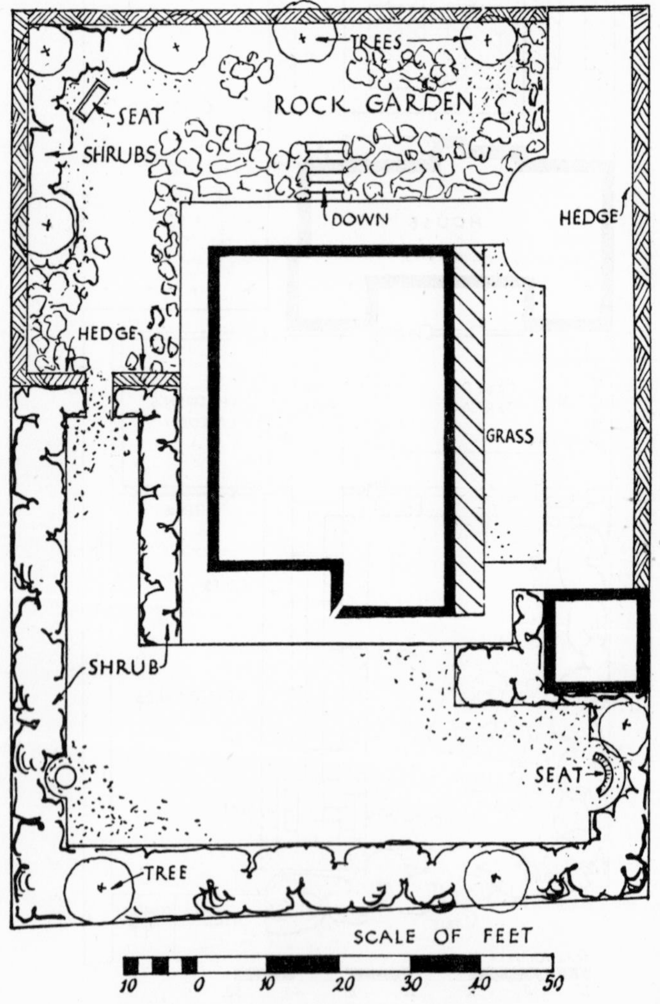

FIG. 12.—A simple layout for a square plot.

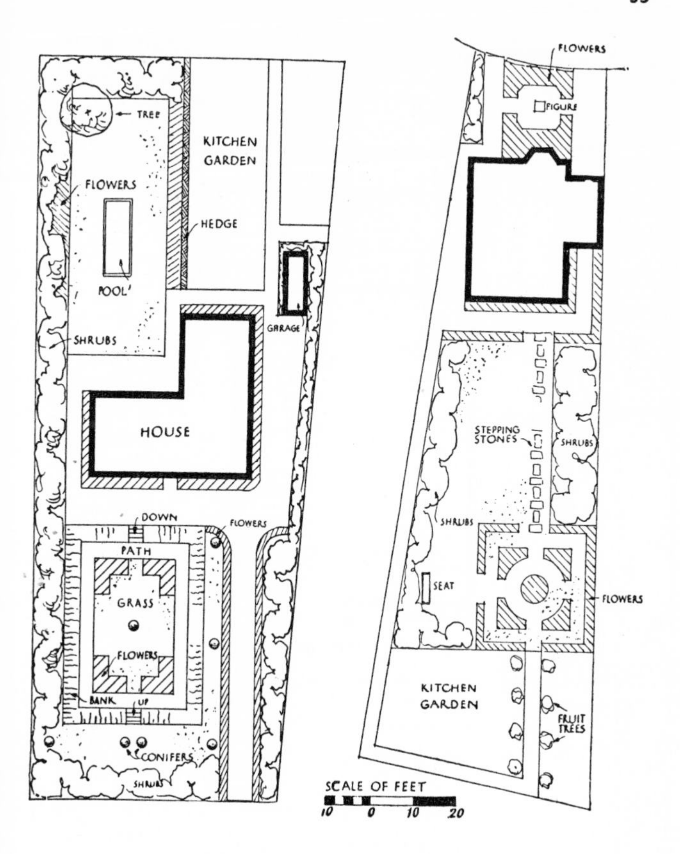

FIG. 13.—Two designs for corner sites.

The corner in both plans is used for a kitchen garden and is screened by hedges and shrubs.

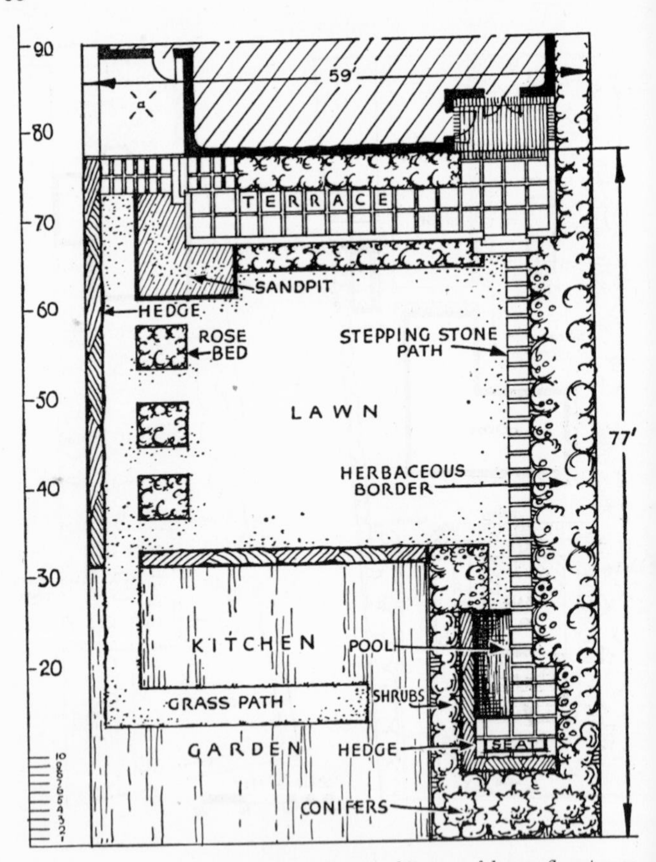

FIG. 14.—A formal design showing the use of large flagstones instead of an ordinary path.

This could be home-made in concrete or York stone in warm buff and yellow tints. Kitchen garden is screened from the house by a Yew hedge.

MATERIALS

Another point on which you must be guided by your own special circumstances is in the choice of materials. An almost limitless choice of materials for path-making, for walls, for rockeries, for garden houses and greenhouses, is available to the modern gardener. Such materials are in all colours, and allow for development of a garden on very characteristic lines. For instance, old red bricks, cobble paving and a little old oak (or stained oak) can be blended in the creation of an old-world garden, with well-heads, wall fountain, pump, or other old-world ornaments. On the other hand, concrete in chosen colours, with coloured pebbles (yellow concrete with blue pebbles, for instance), has been used to create a formal garden that entirely suits the modern concrete house.

Some of these materials may prove expensive, but this should not deter the planner, who can, with a little judicious care and management, design a garden that can be made in gradual stages, so that expenses are spread over a number of years.

CHAPTER IV

BUILDING THE GARDEN FROM THE PLAN

If you have the gift of imagination, you get a big thrill from the actual setting out of the plan on the garden site. You need imagination, for only to you will the queer stumps set here and there over the rough ground have any meaning. Only the painter knows what the picture is to be when he draws his first rough sketches.

Look over the plan, and count up roughly how many pegs you need to set one at each vital point—that is, at each corner of each border and path. Make these pegs ready in advance. Wooden pegs about 18 inches long sharpened at one end, so that they go in without too much trouble, and dipped in white paint or white-wash at the other end so that they show up well, are usually ideal.

For a simple layout it is not a bad idea to provide also a length of string that is knotted at, say, 10 feet or 20 feet, so that you can measure distances easily. A firm stake marked off in feet is also useful. A spade, with which to cut along edges where you intend to make beds and borders, is another layout tool.

Now, suppose your layout is a simple kind, say a path from the back door down one side of the plot, an oblong lawn, straight or curved edged borders, perhaps a trellis screen at the end of the lawn to separate flower garden from a fruit and vegetable patch. Begin by measuring up the path according to the plan, and drive in pegs at each side to show where this will be. Measure up the lawn site, and drive in four or more pegs to indicate this. If you have decided on curved edges to the borders, take your spade, and " nick " out a little drill along the border edge as a guide for digging. Drive in more pegs where the opening to the fruit patch is to come, and where the service paths are to run through the food plots.

WHY PEGS?

All this may seem unnecessary labour, but the truth is that it saves labour afterwards. If by any chance your calculations on paper have been at fault, or if by chance you measure wrongly when you outline a border or path in the garden, you discover it at once if the whole layout is pegged, so that you do not have to make laborious alterations.

Pegging is, naturally, more important when formal gardens are being laid out. I well remember an occasion when two gardens were entered for competition. There seemed little to choose between them, but one of the judges thought one formal layout was a trifle lop-sided. Measurements confirmed his suspicions, and the premier award was lost because beds in one half did not exactly correspond to those in the other half. The garden-maker, a little grieved, explained that he had a good path made before he decided to cut the beds, and he would have had to remake the path to make the beds match exactly. Had he planned *and pegged out* the entire garden before any path-making was done, the irregularity would not have happened.

DIFFERENT LEVELS

Having marked out, with pegs, the positions of the various garden features, tackle the problem of levels. You must deal with these at once, for any soil that is moved from one part of the plot to another, to lower or build up a plot, should be given time to settle before ordinary digging is begun.

Beginners should note here, too, that top soil—the top ten inches or so that one lifts off on a spade blade during digging—is *fertile*, that is, it contains useful soil bacteria and plant food. Below this is soil that is mainly useful in providing an anchor for deep-rooting plants, moisture, and a reserve of plant food that can be tapped when necessary, but is not readily available because of the absence of soil bacteria. This lower subsoil must not be brought to the surface in large quantities, so that if big alterations in levels have to be made, the top fertile layer of soil must first be stripped off, the necessary levelling done to the subsoil, and the fertile soil then replaced in an even layer.

MEET THESE PROBLEMS

Certain problems may be encountered at this stage. Old tree-roots are one. These can be made to decay by treating the stump with chlorate or nitrate of potash, or with strong sulphuric acid: then later they can be burned out (if they are not too near the house). This, however, means a certain amount of delay—six months or so—and the best way to treat old trees on a garden site, if they cannot be retained as a part of the garden picture, is to remove them, root and all, by sheer hard labour!

It may happen that an unsuspected patch of swampy ground is discovered during the process of pegging out the garden. This might be turned to good account by the creation of a small water garden at this point, though more often it will be found that digging will so improve the drainage that the swamp disappears.

More frequently than should be the case, builders carelessly bury the fertile top soil of the original site under a layer of infertile clay, gravel or chalk dug out from the foundations or in putting down drains. This is a serious matter—landscape gardeners regard it as a crime!—and, as already stated, the garden-maker must see that the fertile top soil is once more brought to the surface, or he will be faced with several years of unsatisfactory results.

Sometimes the subsoil, discovered during pegging and laying out, turns out to be useful rockery stone: I know of one garden where the rocky nature of the subsoil was discovered by chance, and this led in time to the formation of what is now a world-famous rock garden.

CONSTRUCTION OF FEATURES

Pegging out is the initial stage—very exciting to the garden-maker, but less interesting to others. We now come to the actual construction of the various artificial features, or the framework of the garden. It is worth while to remark here that although certain artificial features, such as paths, must be made at the very beginning, there are some which can wait until time can be spared for them. The food plots, for example, can be dug over and planted as soon as a hard rolled soil track (for the wheelbarrow) has been prepared as a path. Permanent paths, trellis screens and so on will be added as time permits. On the other hand, a permanent clean and durable path from the house doors is a first essential, and should precede even the digging of the borders.

PATHS

Path-making varies only slightly, according to the use of the path and the kind of surface. The basic principles are the same: the path should be on firm but porous material, so that water does not collect and so that the surface will not sink in places after it is completed. A slight drop at the sides is wise, to allow for water to drain away from the part that gets most wear.

These are the essential steps in path-making:—

1. The area to be made into the path should be stripped of the fertile topsoil, which should be stacked where it can be used for top dressing a border, making a rock garden, or filling pots and boxes in a glasshouse.

2. A layer of coarse, porous material is put down as a base. This must be well rolled before another layer is added.

3. A layer of finer, but still porous material is put over the bottom layer, and again well rolled. Rough bricks, large stones, clinker, cinders, coarse gravel, are useful materials. So are old tins, beaten flat: they must be beaten, or they will gradually subside after the path is made, and cause surface holes.

4. Except on paved paths, where sandy soil and plants are set into the cracks of the paving, a slight camber should be allowed. This can be more pronounced where a gravel surface is intended.

5. Paving-stones can be set in sand or fine cinders, or some concrete can be used below the paving-stones. It is not advisable, from an artistic point of view, for crazy paving to be set entirely in concrete: the result is hard, without the compensating benefit of a perfectly level surface such as one does get if flat tiles are employed. If the crazy-paving-stones are rather small, some may be cemented firmly beneath and in the cracks, while some cracks are left, here and there, mainly towards the sides of the path, for dwarf plants that will soften the appearance.

6. Gravel surfaces should be treated with a waterproof bituminous dressing, over which a second surface of pea gravel, or coloured chips, can be used. Gravel lasts well if so treated, but invariably becomes weedy and uneven if rain can soak into the path.

Two points must be mentioned here: first, if you intend to make drastic alterations on the garden site, so that heavy loads of soil will be wheeled from one part to another, make up the paths only roughly first, and leave the final surfacing until the layout is more developed. And do not let your contractor shoot loads of gravel or other heavy material on to the site of the path you are making: it will inevitably cause the path to sink in that place, and this will result in unevenness later on.

USE OF CONCRETE

Natural stone is excellent for all garden construction, but it is not always available, and gardeners have found that concrete, if well made and used with artistic discretion, is a first-rate substitute. Concrete actually has certain advantages, in that pieces of any desired shape and size can be made, and—a very important point this—additions to the garden features can be made from time to time without any difficulty over *matching* the kind of stone.

Paths can be made of concrete laid down between two strong pieces of wood of equal depth (2 inches) and smoothed off on the surface with a third piece of wood that is shaped to give a camber of about ½ inch for a path 4 feet wide. A more decorative path is made by laying paving-slabs, either to a definite pattern or, if preferred, in the form of crazy paving. To make slabs of this kind for a formal patterned pathway, lay down a frame of 2-inch-thick wood, on a flat part of the garden, and spread sand over the inside soil area, to a depth of ½ to ¾ inch. This sand layer makes it easy to lift the concrete slabs later.

Mix the concrete with one bucket of cement, three buckets of sand and about half a bucket of water, and fill the inside of the frame, levelling the surface with a

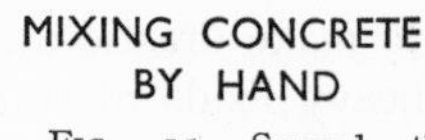

MIXING CONCRETE BY HAND

FIG. 15.—Spread the sand in a flat heap, and dump the cement evenly on top of it. Thoroughly mix the sand and cement by turning over with a shovel until the whole mass is the same colour, free from streaks of brown and grey.

FIG. 16.—Spread the shingle or broken stone, and spread it in a layer on top of the mixed sand and cement. Mix all three ingredients together by turning over with a shovel at least three times, until the coarse material has been uniformly distributed throughout the heap.

FIG. 17.—Sprinkle the water slowly over the heap from a watering-can fitted with a fine rose, stopping frequently to turn over the heap with a shovel. Continuing turning over the heap until the cement, sand, coarse material and water have been uniformly combined into a plastic mass of even colour and consistency.

MAKING AND LAYING PAVING

FIG. 18.—When concrete has been laid one or two hours, cut with a trowel to size required. A straight edge should be used to obtain the lines, and concrete cut to its full depth.

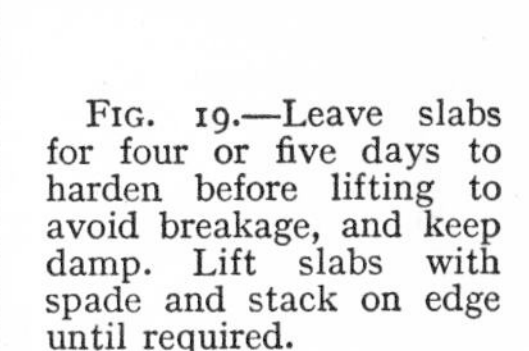

FIG. 19.—Leave slabs for four or five days to harden before lifting to avoid breakage, and keep damp. Lift slabs with spade and stack on edge until required.

FIG. 20.—Joints should be about ½ in. wide, and can be left open as shown, or filled with a coloured mortar to provide a contrast.

CONSTRUCTING A CONCRETE PATH

FIG. 21. — Consolidate ground, remove turf, etc. Lay strong pieces of wood, depth equal to the thickness of concrete required—*e.g.*, 2 ins.—drive in a few pegs to keep the forms in line when the concrete is being placed against them. Fix cross pieces every 5 ft., either of permanent thin soft wood laths or temporary boards of stouter section.

FIG. 22.—Level off by working a piece of wood, shaped to give camber of $\frac{3}{8}$ in. forward over surface, first sawing action, second chopping motion, resting wooden screed on side forms. Protect freshly-placed concrete from drying action of sun and wind by covering with wet sacks for ten days after surface has set sufficiently hard.

FIG. 23.—If the ground is dry, damp the surface before depositing the concrete; wet, spread old newspapers over it, placing the concrete on top of them. Enough concrete should be mixed to complete one bay, and should be deposited within half an hour of commencing mixing. Fill bay, spread with rake, and work to a height about $\frac{1}{2}$ in. above the top of the side forms.

piece of wood worked gradually across the frame, first with a sawing motion and then with an up-and-down chopping motion: this gives a slightly roughened surface that is better for paths than a very smooth surface.

One or two hours later cut through the concrete with a cement trowel, used alongside the straight edge of wood, so that perfectly straight lines result. The concrete can be cut into whatever sized slabs are desired. Do not lift them at once, but four or five days later, when they are hard, lift each carefully with a spade. Stack the slabs on edge until they are required.

An important thing in connexion with mixing concrete is to watch the weather. Slow drying, without exposure to frost, is ideal. If hot weather intervenes, water the concrete daily, and cover it with sacks. If frosty weather is possible, cover the concrete before leaving it for the night.

The mixture given above is useful for small steps and walls, for building into pergolas, pillars and so on. For large paths, steps, thick walls, and many other garden features, shingle may be added to the concrete. It is also possible to buy coloured cements that can be effectively used in certain kinds of garden layout, particularly in small formal town gardens, where variations of colour are particularly appreciated.

TO MAKE STEPS

Steps in a garden add considerably to its charm, and gardens that are on a natural slope can often effectively be planned in terraces, with retaining walls, and ornamental steps to divide the different levels. To make decorative steps, square, or circular in outline, is not difficult. Slabs of fairly small dimensions are easiest if the steps are to be circular in outline—that is, a half circle, or a quarter circle, according to the position of the steps.

The first thing is to fix a stout tall peg into the ground in the central position of the top step. Tie a piece of string to this, and with a pointed stick or other tool, mark the outline of the lowest step; then form the steps roughly in the soil that is the foundation. Build the lowest step first. A mixture as above, with perhaps rather more sand in it, is perfectly suitable for the slabs, which should be about 1½ or 2 inches thick. If 1½ inches, three slabs will be enough, set in a very little concrete, to make the step not more than 5 inches deep. The treads must be 12 inches wide at least, for comfort in use 15 inches is better. The surface of each step consists of larger (or more) pieces of paving, these being allowed to overlap very slightly the slabs that form the risers.

WALLS AND PILLARS

Retaining walls to support soil banks, and prevent rain damage, are built of similar slabs, each being tilted slightly inwards, so that rains run into the soil bank, where plant roots should find a home. In this case, weep holes—that is, holes that penetrate back into the soil—should be left at the wall bottom, to allow for efficient drainage. Plants set at the top of retaining walls of this type quickly begin to creep over the concrete, and form a coloured drapery that is particularly charming.

If walls are made entirely formal in character, with no wall planting, hollow pillars built of slabs with soil filled into the hollow centre can take a small formal evergreen without loss of formality, and small touches of this kind serve to distinguish the "gardener's" layout from that of the house architect.

FORMAL POOLS

A study of the various garden designs in this book will encourage a good many garden-makers to embark

FIG. 24.—Retaining walls are used to edge sunk gardens: they can be built of home-made concrete slabs, and if these are joined by concrete, a few holes should be left here and there, partly as "weep holes," to allow for the escape of water and partly to take pinks, arabis, and other small plants that make the wall a part of the garden.

FIG. 25.—A variety of concrete slabs, tiles, etc., can be built into a low wall with excellent effect.

on the creation of a water garden, formal or semi-formal. These ornamental pools can be made with concrete, but a beginner would be wise to experiment with concrete mixing for other purposes first. Careful and even mixing is particularly necessary in pond construction, for if a pond is once made badly, so that it cracks and loses

FIG. 26.—Concrete slabs can be constructed to edge a formal pool. Grasses and shrubs with coloured foliage form the planting scheme here.

its water, it is very difficult to put it really right again.

To make a small pool, excavate the soil to a depth that will allow for a wall 6 inches thick. Concrete the pond bottom to a depth of 6 inches, using a mixture of one bucket cement, two buckets damp sand, and three buckets shingle, with a little more than half a bucket of water. The next step is very vital: the walls have to be built on to the concrete bottom, and the join between the wall and floor must be very good. For that reason it is wise to leave the edges of the floor bottom quite rough, so that the bond between them and the walls is good. A formwork or frame is built of boards (1-inch boards are ideal) in such a position that it leaves a 6-inch space between the boards and the outer edges of the excavated site. Any method of assembling this is permissible so long as it can be dismantled easily, and to prevent it from adhering overmuch to the concrete, the boards should be well oiled before the concrete is run into the spaces outside the boards. Just before running in this concrete, if the pond bottom has hardened, give the edges a wash with a mixture of equal parts of sand and cement mixed to a creamy consistency. This will help to make a good bond between walls and bottom.

Leave the boards in position for four days, and then remove them and half fill the pond with water. Some of this water may be absorbed by the concrete, and in hot weather some may evaporate, so do not be unduly alarmed if the water appears to have subsided.

The pond edges can be finished off in any manner to suit the style of the garden. Rough lumps of concrete, with grasses and waterside plants set among them, make an informal pool. Smooth slabs set to a formal pattern, the slabs being allowed to project slightly over the edge of the pond (to hide the wall top) make a formal pool.

As a rule the pond must not be stocked with fishes or plants until it has been seasoned—that is, emptied and refilled several times over a period of four to six weeks. There are however, proprietary products for treating new ponds that rapidly make them suitable for animal life. There are also bituminous paints which are available in different colours, for use in ponds.

PERGOLAS

Concrete pergolas are made by building up slabs, made as already described, these being embedded in mortar as in ordinary brick building. The foundations for each pillar are excavated to a depth of 6 inches, and to a size 4 inches larger than the pillars themselves are to be, The excavations are then filled with concrete (as used for the pond bottom) and the pillars are built up above this. Runners across the top are of timber, bolted to the pillars, the bolts being cemented into holes chiselled through the top slabs.

SEATS AND OTHER ITEMS

Cement ends for garden seats, with slots to take the ends of wood strips that form the actual seat: concrete frames for seed-raising: cement tubs and boxes for focal points in the design of formal gardens; cement "temples" for Japanese gardens: concrete edgings to flower borders —these are but a few of the items that will suggest themselves to the gardener who becomes "cement minded". Perhaps, however, I should close this chapter with a word of caution. Never do a second-rate job in concrete. Always mix carefully, and work with care, paying special attention to the artistic appearance of the job. And always soften the appearance, where possible, by the use of plants, or you may find you are not so much using concrete in the garden, as trying to find room for a garden among the concrete!

CONCRETE MIXES FOR THE GARDEN

The concrete mixes given in the following table are based on loose cement weighing 90 lb. per cu. ft., damp sand 84 lb. per cu. ft., shingle 109 lb. per cu. ft., and mixed ballast 130 lb. per cu. ft.

The amount of water given in the last column will in most cases give a mix that can easily be placed and which will give a good finish.

Mix.	Approximate Proportions.			Approximate Proportions. Using Mixed Ballast.		Water to Add.
	Cement (loose). Buckets.	Sand (damp). Buckets.	Shingle. Buckets.	Cement (loose). Buckets.	Mixed Ballast. Buckets.	Buckets.
B	1	3¼	5	1	6	Just over ⅝
C	1	2½	4	1	5	⅝
D	1	2	3	1	4	Just under ⅝
E	1	1¼	2	1	2¾	½
F	1	4	—	—	—	⅝
G	1	3	—	—	—	½
H	1	2	—	—	—	½

In cases where shingle is not obtainable, broken stone, such as crushed granite, may be used, but care should be taken to see that it does not contain an excessive amount of fine dust.

The Mix To Use

Mix.	Suitable for
B	Foundations, footings to walls, filling for garden roller.
C	Garage floors, thick walls.
D	Paths, tanks, pools, pits, steps, garden frames, incinerators.
E	Work of thin section, fence posts, precast steps and kerbs.
F	Concrete rocks, bedding for slabs, filling for paving.
G	Crazy paving, formal paving, small slabs for dwarf walls, pergolas, etc.
H	Rendering to garden pools and tanks.

Maximum Size of Aggregate. For general garden work the material should be graded from ¾ inch to 3/16 inch, but in the case of Mix "B" the maximum size of the stone may be 1½ inches to 2 inches. For work of thin section (Mix "E") the maximum size of stone should not be greater than ½ inch, or less if the work is very thin.

It will be found that mixed ballast is usually graded

QUANTITIES FOR GARDEN WORK: The Materials Required

Mix.	Quantities required per cu. yd. of Concrete.												
	Using Shingle as Coarse Aggregate.								Using Mixed Ballast.				
	Cement.		Sand (Damp).			Shingle.			Cement.		Mixed Ballast.		
	lb.	cwt.	cu. ft.	cu. yd.	cwt.	cu. ft.	cu. yd.	cwt.	lb.	cwt.	cu. ft.	cu. yd.	cwt.
B	392	3·5	14·0	0·52	10·6	21·9	0·81	21·6	405	3·6	27	1·0	31
C	481	4·3	13·8	0·51	10·4	21·3	0·79	20·8	485	4·3	27	1·0	31
D	596	5·2	12·9	0·48	9·8	20·0	0·74	19·4	607	5·3	27	1·0	31
E	813	7·3	11·6	0·43	8·8	18·1	0·67	17·6	880	7·8	27	1·0	31

The Materials Required for Floors, Paths and Walls

Thickness of Slab in Inches.	Quantities per square yard.									
	Mix C.					Mix D.				
	Using Shingle.			Using Mixed Ballast.		Using Shingle.			Using Mixed Ballast.	
	Cement.	Sand (Damp).	Shingle.	Cement.	Mixed Ballast.	Cement.	Sand (Damp).	Shingle.	Cement.	Mixed Ballast.
	lb.	cu. ft.	cu. ft.	lb.	cu. ft.	lb.	cu. ft.	cu. ft.	lb.	cu. ft.
1	13·4	0·38	0·59	13·5	0·75	16·6	0·36	0·55	16·9	0·75
1½	20·0	0·57	0·89	20·2	1·12	24·8	0·54	0·83	25·3	1·12
2	26·7	0·76	1·18	27·0	1·50	33·2	0·72	1·11	33·7	1·50
3	40·1	1·15	1·78	40·5	2·25	49·7	1·08	1·66	50·6	2·25
4	53·4	1·53	2·37	54·0	3·00	66·2	1·44	2·22	67·5	3·00
5	66·8	1·91	2·96	67·5	3·75	82·8	1·80	2·77	84·4	3·75
6	80·2	2·29	3·55	81·0	4·50	99·4	2·16	3·33	101·2	4·50

QUANTITIES FOR GARDEN WORK—*continued*

Materials Required for Small Slabs, Formal and Crazy Paving

Quantities per square yard.

Mix.	½-in. thick.		¾-in. thick.		1-in. thick.		1½-in. thick.	
	Cement.	Sand.	Cement.	Sand.	Cement.	Sand.	Cement.	Sand.
	lb.	cu. ft.	lb.	cu. ft.	lb.	cu. ft.	lb.	cu. ft.
1 to 3 G	—	—	—	—	24	0·8	35	1·2
1 to 2 H	17	0·37	25	0·56	34	0·74	51	1·11

Quantities per square yard.

Mix.	2-in. thick.		3-in. thick.		4-in. thick.		5-in. thick.	
	Cement.	Sand.	Cement.	Sand.	Cement.	Sand.	Cement.	Sand.
	lb.	cu. ft.	lb.	cu. ft.	lb.	cu. ft.	lb.	cu. ft.
1 to 3 G	48	1·6	72	2·4	96	3·2	120	4·0
1 to 2 H	68	1·48	—	—	—	—	—	—

from 1 inch down, but sometimes contains a few large stones; this larger material may be retained for foundations, but should be removed when the concrete is for paths, floors or walls where the thickness is less than 3 inches.

All sand should be graded from $\frac{3}{16}$ inches down, with a good proportion of the larger particles.

Where the Materials Can Be Bought

The materials can be obtained from local builders' merchants, whose depots are generally found in the vicinity of the railway yard.

In the case of coloured cements, some builders' merchants keep a stock, and others will be able to obtain supplies within a few days.

Pigments for colouring ordinary cement can be purchased from paint stores or colour merchants, but inferior qualities should not be used.

Where there are local sand and gravel pits or quarries, supplies of aggregate can usually be obtained direct.

Bedding and Jointing Slabs: Mix F.

When taking out the quantities for a dwarf wall built of small slabs, allowance for the materials required for jointing may be made by taking the overall dimensions of the wall. Moreover for crazy paving and formal paving, where the joints are filled, the gross area of the path should be taken.

Examples

(A) Quantities required for a path 90 ft. long by 3 ft. wide. Using concrete Mix "D"—2 in. thick, using shingle as coarse aggregate.

Area of path in sq. yd. $= \frac{90}{3} \times \frac{3}{3} = 30$ sq. yd.

From table. Quantities per sq. yd. = 33·2 lb. cement, 0·72 cu. ft. sand, 1·11 cu. ft. shingle.

Quantities for 30 sq. yd. = 33·2 × 30 = 996 lb. cement, 0·72 × 30 = 21·6 cu. ft. sand, 1·11 × 30 = 33·3 cu. ft. shingle.

It is best to order to the next cwt. for cement and the next ½ cu. yd. or cu. yd. for the aggregate. Therefore, the following materials should be ordered: 9 cwt. cement, 1 cu. yd. sand, 1½ cu. yd. shingle.

(B) If path is made with precast slabs, 2 in. thick, using Mix "G."

From table. Quantities per sq. yd. = 48 lb. cement, 1·6 cu. ft. sand.

Quantities for 30 sq. yd. = 1,440 lb. cement, 48 cu. ft. sand.

Materials to order—13 cwt. cement, 2 cu. yd. sand.

CHAPTER V

MYSTERIES OF THE SOIL EXPLAINED

On a volcanic island, freshly covered with debris from the action of the volcano, there is no soil, but only layers of ash. For a long time this mass of dusty ash supports no sort of vegetation: it lies on the surface, and is acted on by the weather. Soon a few seeds find their way on to the surface, deposited there by birds or by the winds, and sooner or later a few of these begin to grow. Probably they contrive a somewhat precarious existence, and some of them manage to reach maturity and develop more seeds before they die. The dead plants drop and decay, and gradually become mixed with the ash, and after a few generations of such life and death, the ash begins to take on the nature of soil.

Once plants begin to establish themselves they very quickly make more and more soil for themselves, but the process takes hundreds of years before a sufficient depth of soil exists to support other types of vegetation. We can safely say that the deep, rich, fertile soils found in many parts of this country are the result of thousands of years' growth and accumulation of dying vegetation.

We can define soil, therefore, as a mixture of powdered rock from the original geological formations existing on the earth's surface and decomposed vegetable and animal matter that has become gradually worked into the powdered rock by the action of rains, changing temperatures and the activities of animal life. Owing to the varied nature of local rocks, and also to the variations of climate affecting the growth of vegetable and animal life, soils have become very varied in character. Within a small space such as the British Isles, soils of almost every known type can be found.

As a result of differences of soil, particularly of differences of chemical compounds in the soil, the vegetation of different districts varies. Contours of the land surface affect vegetation too. The flora of a peaty bog, for

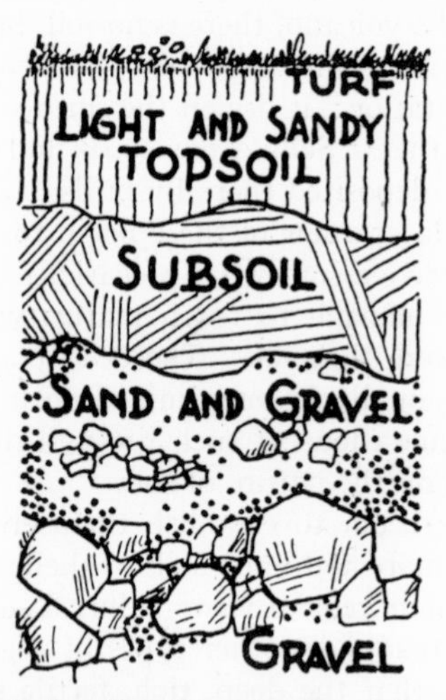

FIG. 27.—Typical section through soil and the layers below.
The top soil is most fertile unless, through building operations, it has been covered over with subsoil.

example, is very different from the flora of the chalk hills. In fact, the thin film of plant life which covers the soil of the earth has definitely been determined by the original character of rocks and soil, with further variations imposed on it by its geographical situation.

In dealing with soil from the horticultural point of view, we describe it according to the type of rock that predominates. The " rock " is the weathered and worn material of the original deposits, sometimes present in finely broken condition, and sometimes present in large masses of unbroken granite or tufa, etc. We are not so much concerned with the hard rocks as with the powdered rock in the soil, and the soils which are the concern of gardeners are chiefly these:—

Sandy Soils. Where sand is plentiful in the soil we call it either a sandy soil or a light soil—" light " referring in this case to its weight. Sandy soil does not hold moisture, and is therefore light in weight.

Clay Soils. Clay is a form of mud, collected by water action. Actually the chief difference between clay and sand is in the size of the soil particles. Clay is fine: it clings to itself (and to the spade) and makes an adhesive mass, and it frequently holds some amount of dead vegetation in it, as well as quantities of water. Clay is found in valleys where rivers bring down material from the hills. There are several types of clay. London clay is different in colour from the boulder clay of the northern counties, and has an entirely different geological origin; but all clay soils have certain characteristics in common, and all behave alike under cultivation.

Chalk Soils. Where chalk forms the subsoil of a district—as, for instance, on the South Downs, or in the limestone district of the Pennine Chain—the surface soil is always more or less of a limy character. The treatment of these soils is the same in all cases, and the type of vegetation found on them in the wild state is generally similar.

Marl. Where limestone has been broken into fragments and has become mixed with both clay and sand, a coarse soil results that is known as marl. Marl is by no means so common as either clay or sand, but it is a soil that is easy to work and one that carries exceedingly good crops.

Humus, or Acid Soil. Humus is actually the decaying vegetation or decaying animal material in soil. Where land is water-logged, a certain type of vegetation develops: this includes mosses, ericas and other "peat-loving" plants. Owing to the stationary character of water in the soil, the decaying vegetation tends to remain where it is, and gradually an accumulation of humus, known as peat, is formed. Sometimes this accumulation is several feet thick. Many of our most fertile potato-growing districts—for example, the Ormskirk district of Lancashire—are on the site of humus-bearing bogland. These soils are known generally as "acid" soils, and to bring them into good condition for many kinds of plants the acidity has to be corrected by digging and liming.

Subsoil. Below the layer which the gardener calls "soil" there is usually a layer of broken rock or sand, which is referred to as the subsoil. This is usually much the same as the top soil, except for the fact that it has in it none of the important humus, or decaying organic matter. It is consequently lighter in colour, and almost infertile, and should not be brought to the surface by the gardener unless for some exceptional reason.

If you go out into any old pasture and cut a turf and then dig down to a depth of, say, 15 inches, you can see for yourself just how these theories work out in practice. You will see that the soil at the top is brownish and full of fibrous material. Beneath this is perhaps 6 inches of soil rather similar, but less fibrous. Under this is the subsoil, which may be clay, marl, chalk or sand. The fertile layer is that near the turf, soil that has been the home of plant life for generations, probably for many thousands of years. Soil of this kind is the real wealth of a nation: it will feed and support humanity, and everything done in the garden, by the gardener, should be designed to conserve and make the best use of this rich and precious heritage.

SOIL DRAINAGE

Now let us turn our attention to the work we have to do in order to make our soils as useful to us as they can become. We have already noticed that where soil is water-logged certain classes of plant thrive—ericas and bog plants generally. Other plants (most of our food crops) set out in this water-logged soil would merely decay and become useless. One of our first jobs in gardening, therefore, is to attend to the drainage of our land. Over a great part of the British Isles land-drains are already in existence, and invariably where building is done on a large scale, the question of land drainage has already been given some attention. There are, however, a good many gardens where drainage is not free enough for the soil to remain in good condition whatever the weather, and in any garden some attention must be given to drainage. Just how much work needs to be done in this respect can be discovered by a few simple tests.

First, assuming that the garden is in a district where good main drains are present, make a simple test in this way. Dig out a hole in what appears to be the lowest part of the garden—say about 2 feet square and 15 inches deep. Leave it open during a period of heavy rain, and note whether the rain clears away from the hole rapidly after rainfall ceases, or whether it remains for a week or two in the hole. If it remains, the probability is that your subsoil is of clay, and that deep digging, combined with general soil improvement, as will be described below, will effect a cure. In certain cases, however, the hole may appear to become the " sump " for water draining off a neighbour's garden, or a neighbouring hillside. If this should be the case, a serious drainage problem arises which should be tackled before any gardening is attempted.

To drain any plot of ground is a comparatively simple matter if there is a ditch or main drain into which the surplus water can be conveyed. If there is nothing of this kind, a garden can be drained into a sump—*i.e.*, a very deep hole which is filled to within 18 inches of the surface with large stones, bricks, clinker and other open, porous material. In some gardens it has been found convenient to construct an artificial pool in the lowest part of the grounds, and to drain surplus water from other areas into the pool and its surrounding bog-garden.

So rarely does a very serious problem arise that we shall not deal here with anything beyond the scope of the small garden owner. If, however, a plot of ground must be drained, where it is proposed to make a lawn, this method can be adopted. First dig a trench across the lawn, preferably from the end that is driest to the end that is wettest. It will be noted that if any excavation has to be done to prepare a level patch for the lawn, the wettest part will usually be where the ground was dug from the hillside. A trench from corner to corner of a rectangular lawn is satisfactory, and from this first trench a series of side trenches should be dug, herring-bone fashion. The trenches should slope at the bottom from about 1 foot deep to about 2 feet deep, or just sufficiently for the water to be carried away to one end. At this end the sump should be made, or a drain laid that will take the water to the main drains.

In refilling the trench, it is usually sufficient to put in first a 6- or 8-inch layer of coke-breeze or clinker, or other equally porous material: then to refill with the original soil. If this soil is heavy, sticky clay, mix some sand or grit with it as it is thrown in, or the drains will be almost useless.

Trenches cut and refilled in this way will drain soil to a distance of about 15 feet on each side.

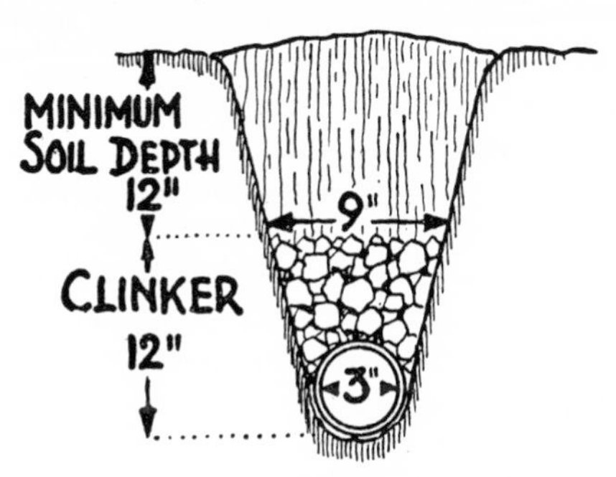

FIG. 28.—Method of inserting agricultural land drains.

Note the use of clinker covering, to prevent soil washing into the drain.

DRAINAGE BY CULTIVATION

We must repeat that in most small gardens no special trench-drains are needed. If ground is dug in such a way that the subsoil is regularly broken well, down to a depth of 2 feet, there will be little difficulty over faulty drainage in the food-plots. Path drainage is also a problem that is usually solved by correct path-laying, allowing a slight camber on rolled paths, whether of gravel or grass, and using plenty of porous material under paths of paving-stone or tile.

CHEMICAL CONTENTS OF SOIL

Ignoring soil contents that may not be of use to a plant, here are the chief elements which are necessary to plant life, and which it must obtain either from the soil and the moisture therein or from the air: nitrogen, oxygen, calcium, carbon, hydrogen, iron, magnesium, phosphorus, potassium, sulphur. There are other substances which form part of the plant, but as they are generally present in soil, they, too, can be ignored.

Of the elements mentioned, carbon, hydrogen and oxygen can be, and are, absorbed by the plants from air and water alone. Calcium is often present, but is usually also supplied in the form of lime-dressings, and in the vegetable garden and fruit-patch these dressings are required every year, or (heavier dressings) every two years. Iron, too, is usually present in sufficient quantities, and rarely should the gardener supply additional iron except for special purposes. Magnesium and sulphur are nearly always present in soils. The only remaining substances that we have to consider, therefore, are those that form the basis of commercial fertilisers —nitrogen, phosphorus and potassium. These substances tend to become used up by growing plants, and unless they are applied again, naturally (by plant decay, as in Nature) or artificially, healthy plant life cannot be maintained.

PHYSICAL NATURE OF SOIL

Before discussing in detail the question of artificia fertilisers, let us again turn our attention to the construction of soil. We have seen that soils differ, that they are made by the decay of plant and animal life and the weather action on original rocky formations. We should remind ourselves, too, that what we call the "texture" of the soil is vastly important in gardening. The top spit of cultivated soil is generally friable and easy to dig, rake or hoe. Such soil is able to hold moisture without being water-logged, and, what is very important, it is able, like a sponge, to soak up from lower soil layers a quantity of water, raised by capillary attraction from a very great depth. Experiments have been made with various kinds of soil in long tubes showing that good, cultivated garden soil, containing a fair proportion of fibrous matter, will raise water by this means from a much greater depth than will either pure sand or solid clay. Since plants can absorb plant food only through the root-hairs in the form of a solution, it will easily be recognised that everything depends on the presence of water through the soil, and any cultivation that will make the soil uniformly moist without being water-logged (*i.e.*, airless) will prove beneficial to plant life.

LIFE IN THE SOIL

There is another and equally important reason for improving soil texture so that moisture and air can both play their part below the surface. Soil is not just a mass of dead matter. Decay does not mean a cessation of life in the soil: soil organisms are busy converting insoluble plant foods into soluble foods. One set of mirco-organisms converts sulphate of ammonia into nitrites, another then converts these into nitrates; the nitrates are soluble and can be absorbed by the root-hairs when they are dissolved in the water of the soil.

This sort of microscopic life goes on all the time in the soil, particularly in soil that is constantly aerated by digging. That is why deep digging in early winter is so important: the organisms have longer to do their work on the manure or compost that is dug into the soil, and they are able to penetrate to a greater depth in dug soil, and so render fertile more of the soil than if digging is delayed until spring.

MAKING SOIL FERTILE

Soil fertility is a wide term, and means just the power of the soil to support plant life. This, as we have seen, depends on a variety of circumstances—on the physical condition of the soil, on the work that has been or can be done by micro-organisms in the soil, and on the chemical content of the soil. When, therefore, the gardener determines to make his soil fertile, it is not enough merely to add to the soil a certain amount of each of the plant foods, even if he can (as modern chemistry would certainly permit, since it does this in the case of soilless culture—see Chapter VI) add these foods in solution ready to be absorbed by the roots. The digging and hoeing that are part of the gardener's job are essential because the plants must not only have the food, but must have a root system capable of taking up the food, and in uncultivated land a large root system cannot develop as it can in well-dug soil.

What, then, are the practical ways to treat garden soil to attain the desired condition of soil fertility? First, the soil should be well dug every autumn, or, in the case of plots cultivated intensively (*i.e.*, crops quickly following each other), the ground should be double dug once in two years, and turned over to the depth of one spit whenever it happens to be unoccupied by crops.

Double digging, as the name implies, means digging to double the depth of the spade-blade, the top layer being completely turned over, while the under layer is broken up so that it becomes porous and assists capillary action, by which the plants can obtain water in dry weather. The simple way to double dig is to open up a series of trenches, filling the first with the material dug from the second, the second with material dug from the third, and so on. A good plan is to divide in half lengthways the plot to be dug, cut out a trench across the end of one half, and wheel the soil removed to a position near the same end of the other half-plot. Thus it will be easy to fill the last trench with soil taken from the first.

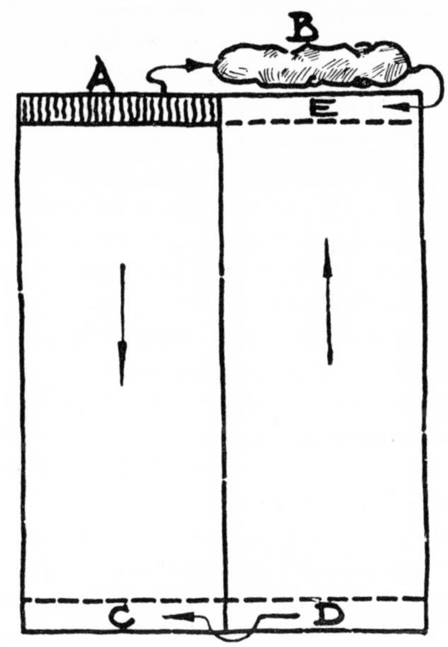

FIG. 29.—Best method of digging a vegetable plot.

Divide the area into two, as shown in the above diagram. Beginning at A a trench is opened, the soil from which is placed at B; the soil from D is filled into trench C and, at the completion, the soil at B is filled into end trench E.

FIG. 29A.

Double digging is the method of breaking up subsoil without bringing it to the top. In the above diagram the soil is removed from trench A; at B the subsoil is broken up, then the soil from trench C is placed on the top of B and D is then broken up.

In double digging, after each trench is opened, the worker gets into the trench and breaks up the subsoil, using a large digging fork for the purpose. At the same time, compost from the compost pit, or stable manure, or other organic matter, partially decayed, is thrown into the open trench, and mixed into the top layer of soil. This again assists in retaining moisture and food in the soil.

Fertilisers are applied as a rule to the soil surface, and either allowed to wash in with the rains, or, if they are not readily soluble chemicals, they are lightly forked or hoed into the surface. The amount of each fertiliser needed, and the kind of fertiliser needed, depend on the amount of compost available, and its content, and the kind of crops that are grown. The question which of two available fertilisers to use is generally determined by the physical nature of the soil, and of course by the cost of the fertiliser. We have already seen that the plant foods that concern the gardener most particularly are nitrogen, phosphates, potash and lime. Let us take them singly.

NITROGEN

About four-fifths of the air we breathe is nitrogen, yet plants are not able to extract and use this nitrogen, and without the help of micro-organisms, acting in the soil, nitrogen would not be available to the roots. Nitrogen can be supplied by applications of nitrate of soda, sulphate of ammonia, calcium cyanamide (Nitrolim), nitrate of potash (saltpetre) or nitro-chalk. Sulphate of ammonia, a by-product of the gas industry, nitro-chalk and nitrate of soda, are the most common fertilisers sold to supply nitrogen to garden soil. Nitrate of soda and sulphate of ammonia are very quick-acting, and never used in autumn digging, but only as dressings in spring and during the active growing season. Nitro-chalk should also be used through the growing season, and has the advantage that some lime is present, so that it is useful on soils inclined to acidity. (Only one of these nitrogenous fertilisers is required, of course!)

The amount of nitrogen needed can be decided on with regard to the amount used in the compost heap (if any) and the type of crops. Nitrogen builds up a plant: it makes it grow large and leafy, and in doing this, it somewhat delays flower production. Nitrogenous food, therefore, is wanted specially by green food crops, salads, and in smaller quantities by all other garden plants.

PHOSPHATES

Both nitrates and phosphates are present to some extent in compost or farm manure, but it is generally essential to supply additional phosphates for most parts of the garden. Sources of phosphatic food are basic slag, superphosphate of lime, phosphate of potash and bones—*i.e.*, bonemeal or boneflour. Bones and basic slag are slow-acting, and are used in winter digging. Superphosphate of lime and phosphate of potash are quick-acting, and used in spring and during active growth. Basic slag is best on heavy, rich soil; bonemeal is good in preparing soil for roses and fruit trees, where the soil will not be dug again during the life of the plant. Bonemeal is also useful in herbaceous borders. Phosphate of potash is particularly useful on pot plants of all kinds.

POTASH

Seaweed, burnt clay from under the bonfire, wood-ash, and bird-droppings are all good sources of potash. Commercial potash fertilisers include kainit, sulphate of potash, muriate of potash, phosphate of potash and nitrate of potash.

The effect of potash is to make flowers and fruits a better colour, leaves a deeper green, all plants healthier and better able to resist disease; and potash deficiency is perhaps the most frequent cause of unidentified trouble in the amateur's garden. Most potash fertilisers are used in autumn, as certain impurities are present (in kainit, for instance) that need to be washed out before the growing season. Phosphate of potash and nitrate of potash can be used during the growing season, and particularly on valuable pot plants.

Further reference to fertilisers for special purposes will be given in later chapters, but as a general guide for quantities, etc., we give here a brief list of manures and fertilisers, together with the quantities to be used on each square yard of ground. These quantities should not generally be exceeded, and the novice should remember that ground treated in autumn with a phosphatic fertiliser will not need more fertiliser of this class in spring.

Finally, for the owner of a small garden and limited storage space, who cannot conveniently store and use a large quantity of separate chemicals, here is a recipe for a good all-round fertiliser that can be safely used in all parts of the garden. It is familiarly known as the one-three-one mixture, and consists of one part sulphate of ammonia, three parts superphosphate, and one part sulphate of potash.

To prevent caking during storage (if the mixture is kept for long periods) one further part of coarse bone-meal may be added.

NITROGENOUS FERTILISERS

Sulphate of ammonia . .	½ oz. per square yard.
Nitrate of soda . . .	½ oz. per square yard.
Calcium cyanamide . .	½ oz. per square yard if used in conjunction with organic refuse.
Nitro-chalk . . .	2 oz. per square yard.

PHOSPHATIC FERTILISERS

Superphosphate of lime	2 oz. per square yard.
Basic slag	2 to 4 oz. per square yard.
Bonemeal or boneflour	Up to 3 oz. per square yard.

POTASH FERTILISERS

Sulphate of potash	Up to 1 oz. per square yard.
Kainit	2 oz. per square yard.
Slaked lime	Up to ½ lb. per square yard.

Apply to the surface soil after digging: buried too deeply, soluble fertilisers are lost by leaching.

CHAPTER VI

SOILLESS CULTURE

THE most remarkable horticultural development of recent years has been the discovery and practice of hydroponics, or soilless culture of plants. It is no new idea to grow plants in cultural solutions: botanical experiments on these lines have been carried out for a long time, and over a century ago laboratory experiments of this kind proved the nutritional requirements of plants and the effect of different chemicals. It is new, however, for gardeners to attempt the culture of plants in chemicals and water only for commercial purposes, and it is only recently that full growth to maturity has been found possible and practicable to food producers.

Hydroponics can be called an adaptation of the early laboratory methods of growing plants in chemicals. With specially constructed tanks and other equipment, it has been found commercially profitable to grow plants in water and chemicals alone: in fact, so successful has the idea proved that in the United States of America large producers of flowers, vegetables and salads have given up the use of soil in glasshouses and have entirely adopted the soilless method of production.

The pioneer of this new horticultural science is Dr. W. F. Gericke, who has written the standard text-book on the subject, and who is better qualified than any other experimenter to write on hydroponics. A great many followers have, however, made interesting experiments in the practical application of Dr. Gericke's theories, and there is already a fairly large output of literature on the subject.

Soilless culture is of particular interest to the man who wishes to learn the science of gardening, whether he continues to practise this method or not, for soilless culture demonstrates very spectacularly the different plant needs and the effects of different feeding on plants.

TWO METHODS

There are two practical methods of using chemical solutions alone to aid plant-growth. One is to use water, with chemicals or vermiculite added, and for this method plants must be suspended in a basket or trap above the solution. The other is to use sand, gravel or other sterile material to which the nutrient solutions are added. The sand method has several advantages over the water method. The plants have a medium for anchorage, and their cultivation in sand is generally less troublesome than in water alone.

The cultivation of plants without soil reveals interesting facts as to their chemical requirements. It has been found, for instance, that in addition to the recognised plant-foods that concern the ordinary gardener, a number of other elements are needed. It would not, in other words, be sufficient to add nitrate of soda, superphosphate and potash to water, and plants grown in such a solution would soon fail.

CHEMICALS REQUIRED

The following formula for soilless culture is composed from chemicals sold as fertilisers:—

	Grams.	Grains.
Superphosphates (monocalcium phosphate plus calcium sulphate)	7·0	108
Sodium nitrate . . .	7·6	117
Magnesium sulphate . .	12·3	190
Potassium chloride . . .	4·7	72
Water	75 gallons.	

To this is added a teaspoonful of trace elements made up as follows:—

3·2 grams, or 49 grains, each of boric acid, manganese sulphate, zinc sulphate, dissolved in 64 oz. of water.

Messrs. Ellis & Swaney, the American experimenters, state that this formula has proved successful with the culture of potatoes, tomatoes, radishes and lettuces, in addition to carnations, gladiolus and tuberous begonias.

PRACTICAL APPLICATION

The beginner in soilless experimental work can adapt the methods of the commercial growers to the cultivation of a few plants. For instance, half a dozen tomato plants could be grown in a water-tight window-box, 4 feet long by 1 foot wide and 6 inches deep. Sand can be used to take the plants, and the sand should first be washed with a little acid (5 per cent. hydrochloric) and then washed again with clear water. It is important that the box used should be painted inside with a bitumastic paint. Zinc boxes have been tried, but it was found that the zinc has a toxic effect on the water.

A method of supplying the tank with moisture must be arranged. This can be either by the drip method or by flooding or submergence. The drip method means that water containing the required chemicals is supplied at a rate only equal to that of the plant in using up the solution, so that there will never be a surplus. The flooding method means that the tank is periodically filled with cultural or nutrient solution, and the surplus is allowed to drain back into a reservoir.

A simple home-made contrivance that enables the second method to be easily adopted and applied is illustrated in the following diagram.

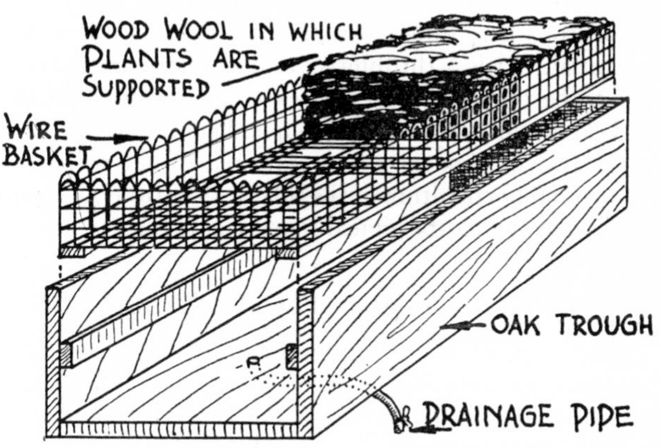

FIG. 30.—Method of constructing window-box for soilless culture.

The inner lining of box should be painted with bitumen to prevent leakage and the toxic effect of some woods upon the water solution.

TYPES OF PLANTS TO GROW

Almost every type of plant has been and can be grown by soilless culture. In experiments carried out at Reading and elsewhere, crops of 5 lb. and 6 lb. of tomatoes per plant have been obtained by soilless culture. This method holds immense possibilities for the future. By its adoption, large tracts of desert, at present uncultivated, may and will become fertile. This immense store of latent possibilities is what makes soilless culture so fascinating today. Even such crops as potatoes have been tried, and they have been known to give 800 per cent. greater yield by soilless culture than by ordinary soil culture.

Soilless culture of plants in the British Isles is certainly still in the experimental stage, in so far that presence or absence of sunshine, and different atmospheric conditions, affect crops here differently even in districts not widely separated. It is a thrilling as well as instructive experience to be taking part in new experimental work of this kind, especially when it is remembered that a horticultural revolution may be taking place that will make commercial horticulture of the future an entirely different thing from the old-fashioned market-gardening.

BOX AND COX AND PLANT ASSOCIATIONS

Another point about soilless culture is that crops can be grown in close association, or in rapid succession. Potatoes, tomatoes and celery, for instance, have been made to play Box and Cox and share the same bed in quick succession through the year. Association of plants in the cultural tank affords opportunities for close study, and it may easily be found that the present high cropping standards become even more striking if and when plants that help each other are grown in the same solution.

If you are out to teach yourself gardening, here is the type of experiment that you might undertake.

Peas or beans could be grown in the same tank as potatoes, and, for comparison, the two crops could also be grown separately, but under similar conditions. The effect of the nitrogen-forming pea or bean root (most legumes have the power of fixing nitrogen in root nodules, thus leaving the soil richer in nitrogen, if the roots are left in the soil when the tops are cleared) would be seen in the results of the potato crop. It has been claimed by the old-type gardener that peas grown in conjunction with potatoes in soil give a larger potato crop, and it would be interesting to note if this happens in the case of soilless culture.

Other such experiments will occur readily to the gardener who has both soil and tanks under his care.

It is interesting to note that biochemists claim that there is no difference in the food value of crops well grown whether by soilless culture or ordinary methods. Another interesting point is that plants grown by the soilless culture method appear to thrive for many years, not just for a single season. The writer has seen carnations that, after five generations of soilless culture, were equal in substance and quality to any he has seen in ordinary soil.

The advantages of soilless culture are these:—

1. No heavy digging or ploughing is needed.
2. No heavy wheeling of manure on to the plot is necessary.
3. No hoeing or weeding has to be done in summer.
4. The control of disease and pests is simplified.

In short, all the factors which influence the health and well-being of plants under ordinary soil culture (apart, of course, from weather conditions and latitude) are completely under the control of the gardener in the case of soilless culture.

Developed to the stage in which automatic, mechanical methods of changing waters, adding chemicals, aerating water, etc., are available in large glasshouses, manual labour is reduced to an absolute minimum.

FOR SMALL EXPERIMENTS

The beginner can make his first experiment in this way. First the tank and sand should be prepared as already described. A nutrient solution should also be prepared, nutrient chemicals can be purchased ready-mixed.

Tomato seedlings (from a nursery, if seeds cannot be conveniently raised) should be obtained, and before being planted in the sand, they should be washed free of all old soil. The solution should be used to moisten the sand, but surplus solution should be drained away, so that air can also reach the roots. As required, the solution is given instead of ordinary water, and will, naturally, be needed in increasing quantities as the plants develop.

Grown in this way, the plant roots will get the air they need. If a tank of water, with a basket holding the plants (set usually in moss or other medium that will give anchorage to the plant), is used, aeration is done laboriously by the grower, by raising the basket, until the roots are out of the solution, and then lowering them again. This may need to be done twice daily to keep the plants in good condition, and for this reason alone, the sand method is preferable.

For further details of soilless culture the reader will naturally turn to the ever-increasing volume of books that are being written on the subject. A little experiment or two on simple lines will, however, prove a better teacher than most of the books.

CHAPTER VII

SIMPLE GARDEN STRUCTURES AND HOW TO MAKE THEM

AMONG garden structures can be included garden houses, and similar useful-for-pleasure features. I do not propose to deal with all of them, but merely with the structures that are of prime use to the gardener in the cultivation of crops.

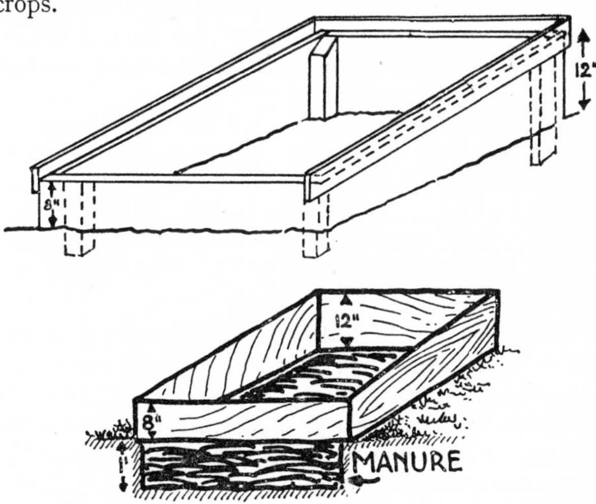

FIG. 31.—Method of constructing a box frame on a hotbed. 2 in. × 2 in. corner-pieces inside the frame would give added strength.

The cold frame is perhaps the most useful of all structures. It consists of a (usually) portable framework of wood, rather like the sides of a box, but with two sloping sides. Over this fits a "light"—*i.e.* a window-frame which either opens on a hinge or, more conveniently, slides across the frame, so that it can be used when required to shelter plants in the frame, and removed at will when more air and sunlight are wanted by the plants. A glance at the illustration will show how such a frame can be made, by any handyman. The frame should be put in such a position in the garden that the "light" slopes towards the south, so that the maximum amount of light reaches the plants.

A garden frame can be artificially heated. Alternatively, it can be used over a hotbed, which is merely a raised bed formed of fresh animal manure and leaves, with a layer of good soil over the top. Such a soil bed must be allowed to lose some of its heat before use, to allow plants to be set out in the soil, but even before the heat has dropped the hotbed and frame can be used: boxes are filled and seeds sown, and these boxes, set on bricks so that air circulates under them, can be kept in the frame over the hotbed. By the time the seeds germinate, the soil of the hotbed is generally ready to receive the seedlings.

A frame without hotbed or artificial heat is a useful protection in early spring, and such a frame can be set over a bed of ash or clinker. Boxes and pots of seeds are then set in the frame as desired, frosts being excluded by the use of mats over the lights when cold nights occur.

Greenhouses are of several types. The lean-to is the simplest, and takes up the least garden space, but it is only really suitable for the walls that face south. Greenhouses can be heated by boilers using coke, oil or gas as fuel, or they can be electrically heated. Electricity is also used to heat the soil of frames, and both gas and electrical heating apparatus can be automatically controlled, thus lessening the need for labour.

Propagating Pits are, as their name suggests, pits dug out below the general soil-level, and are usually heated by the pipes that serve the greenhouse and frames.

A small greenhouse and one or two frames are, in my opinion, useful adjuncts to the home garden, for they allow for seedlings to be raised early under glass, and for crops such as tomatoes and cucumbers to be grown over a long period, instead of just during the summer months.

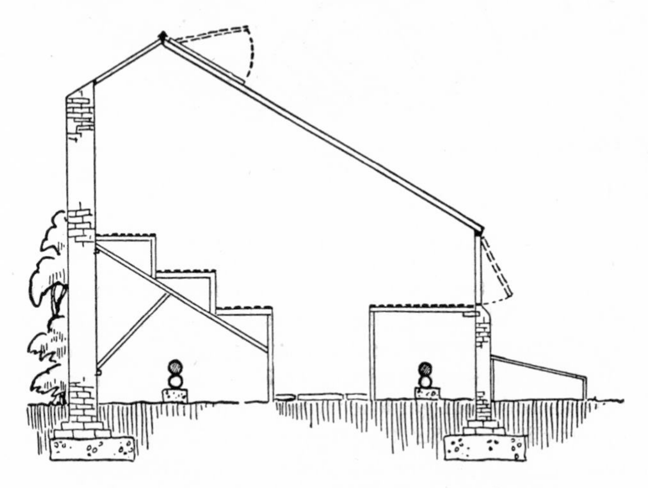

FIG. 32.—Section of a simple lean-to greenhouse.

Note the provision of top and bottom ventilators and the cold frame along the front of the greenhouse.

Cloches are also useful to the food producer. These are portable glass protections, in various shapes, which can be used over plants that are growing in the open ground. They are set in position over early sowings of peas, lettuces, etc., then possibly moved to shelter straw-berries, and later on used to protect late-sown French beans, or similar crops. Their use cannot be exhaustively treated here, but every gardener who wishes to learn by experience is advised to purchase some cloches, and to discover for himself how much can be done by the use of these simple protective aids.

FIG. 33.—Cloches are used to protect early and late crops and play an important part in intensive cultivation.

FENCES AND SCREENS

A word or two must also be said concerning fences and screens. All plants, like animals, are more tender when they are young than when they are mature. Wattle hurdles and similar portable screens are therefore very useful to the gardener who tries to fight the vagaries of our climate. Set temporarily on the windy side of a row of seedlings, hurdles make a protection that will frequently save the lives of the plants and will invariably speed up growth.

Permanent screens, if of wood, should receive attention at the hands of the gardener every year.

A coat of creosote is the best treatment for wood outdoors, but creosote is not liked by plants, and while it is drying off no plants should be allowed to touch the wood that has been treated.

Wood that is painted, such as the wood of the greenhouse (unless cedar wood, untreated, is used), should

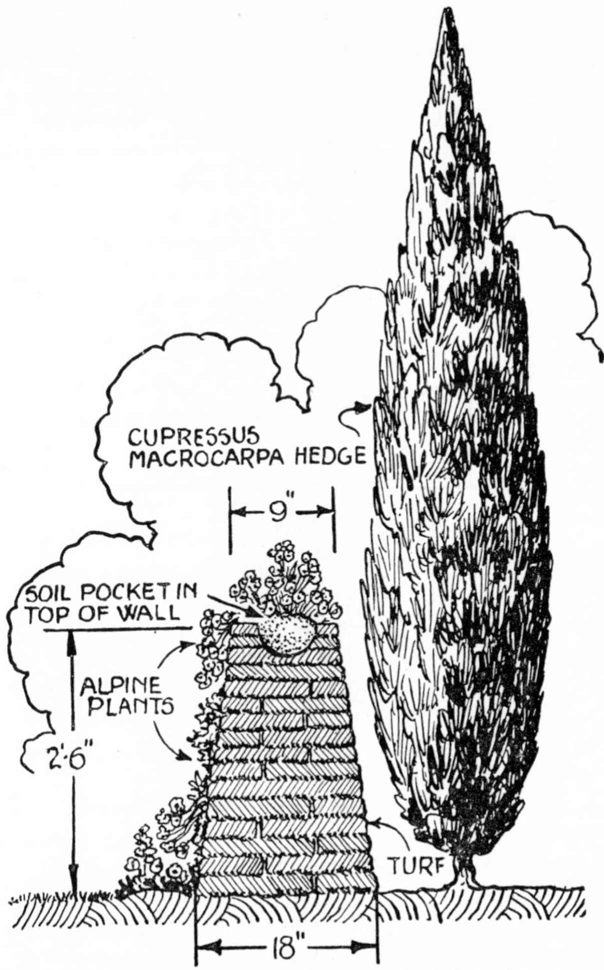

FIG. 34.—Screen wall built of turf obtained from lawn areas that have been converted for vegetables. Built up like this and planted with quick-growing alpines, it will give a rapid screening effect.

always be kept in good condition, for DECAYING WOOD IS A DANGER TO THE GARDENER. It harbours pests of all kinds.

CONSTRUCTION OF POPULAR GARDEN STRUCTURES

A study of the illustrations of screens, arches and other features given here will give the handyman a sufficient guide to their construction. There are, however, certain rules that affect these structures, which must be obeyed if they are to give really good service *outdoors*.

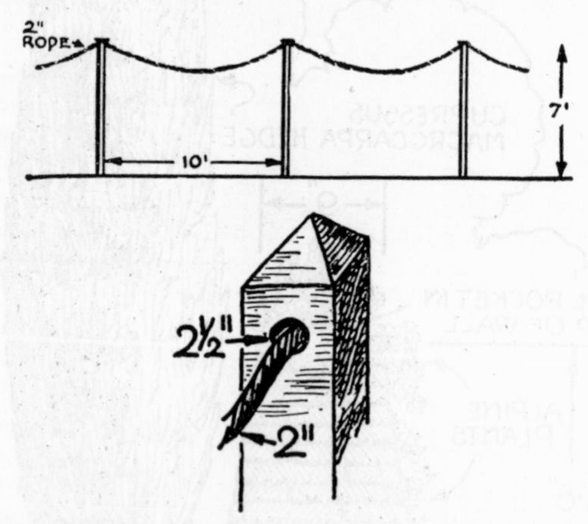

FIG. 35.—Method of fixing rope to a post.

All wooden supports that go into the ground should be embedded in concrete. Wood, of whatever kind is selected, will first decay at the ground level or below it, where moisture constantly collects. If the wood is embedded in concrete, this decay is avoided. The concrete should be deep enough to make a firm foundation, and the top surface of the concrete that surrounds each wooden post should be finished with an outward, downward slope, so that rain is carried rapidly away from the wood. This applies whether the wood is sawn and planed or left with its own rough surface: in the latter case, however, it is advisable to peel off the bark from the lower portion of the support before the concrete is laid down.

In erecting screens, only the stout supporting posts should actually touch the soil: the boards that are nailed to the supports are best raised an inch or two, so that moisture does not collect on them and cause decay at the foot of the fence.

FIG. 36.—Trellis work, constructed in oak, with foot squares. This makes a simple screen for climbing fruits, roses, or shrubs.

If a pergola is erected, the posts should be usually about eight feet apart across the pathway and eight feet apart down the length, nine or ten feet high, and with crossbars every eight feet to coincide with the spacing of the supporting posts. It is generally desirable that the crossbars should extend a foot each way beyond the posts, and that the posts themselves should go down two feet into the ground, this portion being first creosoted and then embedded in concrete.

Timber for a pergola of this proportion should be from six to nine inches square.

The range of materials that can be used for pergola construction is so extensive that we cannot here deal fully with the subject. Posts can be of stone, concrete slabs, rustic wood, brick and tile, or natural rock. Runners and crossbars can also be of various types. Where rustic wood of rather thin larch poles is the chosen material, the uprights and crossbars can be arranged in pairs, to give greater stability, and all kinds of other variations will suggest themselves to each gardener, according to his circumstances.

FIG. 37.—A decorative use of rectangular paving stones laid flush with the grass to allow for the use of the mower. Such stones take the wear in places where there is constant traffic across a lawn.

Garden seats can be home-made, or purchased: their setting in the garden must be chosen with care according to the type of garden and the type of seat. Where any kind of permanent seat is selected, the site should be prepared so that the feet will always rest on reasonably dry ground. A flat stone or two dropped into the grass where the feet will rest is enough for a seat set on a lawn, but care should be taken to see that the stones

FIG. 38.—Effective and simple and very enduring, is this method of supporting climbing roses

FIG. 39.—Wrought iron gates give a rare dignity to any garden scheme.

FIG. 40.—A rose arch is within the capacity of most gardeners.

FIG. 41.—Dovecote and thatched garden shelter.

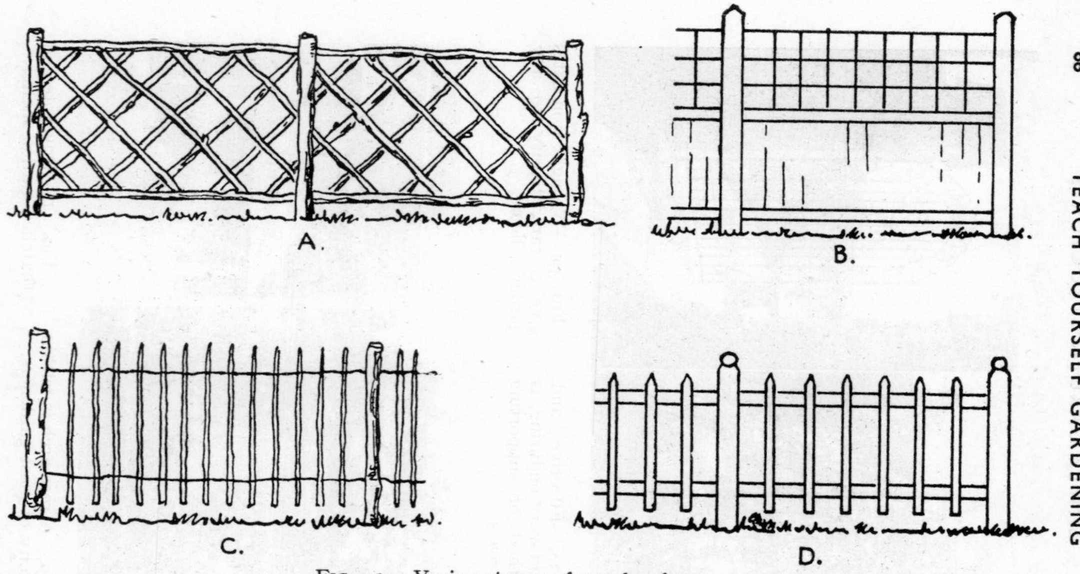

FIG. 42.—Various types of wooden fences.

(A) Rustic.
(B) Square trellis and boards in oak. No paint or preservative is used, butt ends of the posts only are treated before fixing.
(C) Chestnut pale fencing.
(D) A simple wooden fence painted in white, brown or green.

are set a little higher than the lawn level—a slope of an inch or two up towards the seat is unnoticeable, but is sufficient to divert heavy showers.

One last point—every special garden feature, such as a dovecote or rustic bridge, quickly becomes a centre of attraction to visitors, and it is of vital importance that the approach to each should be specially considered. A few stepping-stones to take the extra foot traffic will prevent that worn track across a lawn which is such a common disfigurement.

GREENHOUSE COMPOSTS, ETC.

For fuller treatment of greenhouse and frame gardening, other chapters and a wider library must be referred to, but here is a brief list of potting-soils, etc., that the gardener ought to keep for use under glass:—

Peat.
Loam (decayed turves).
Leaf-mould.
Sand.
Charcoal.
Mortar rubble.
Decayed manure.
Fertilisers.
Insecticides, including soil fumigants, and sterilisers.

CHAPTER VIII

RAISING NEW PLANTS

PERHAPS it is the commercial instinct for a good bargain that is responsible, or perhaps it is the meeting with Nature's deepest mysteries that exerts its fascination; but whatever the cause, one thing is certain, that every gardener loves to raise new plants. There are a great many ways in which he can do this, and there is something to be said for each method. As a general rule we adopt the method that will give us good results in our small gardens with a minimum of effort.

What we call good results are naturally a little different from the good results that a commercial raiser of new plants is out to achieve. He wants new and outstanding varieties that have not hitherto been seen or sold. We probably want a good show of colour, or a good crop of vegetables or fruit. The commercial grower can afford to raise a thousand new plants if one of them proves a "winner" in the novelty class. We want uniformity in our plants, and cannot waste our limited space in growing plants of which a large proportion will be useless.

Now let us see how these general principles work out in practice.

There are, as already stated, many different ways to raise plants, but they all fall into one of two different groups: *seed-raising*, and *vegetative reproduction*. In the case of seed-raising, the germ of the new plant, which is in the seed, is the product of sexual reproduction—that is, the seed has two parents: the mother plant from which it was taken and on which it grew and ripened, and the father plant (often unknown), which provided the pollen that fertilised the seed and made it able to develop and ripen. A seed, therefore, is a new baby, inheriting some of its characteristics from one plant and some from another plant. It may, as our own babies, inherit more from one parent than from the other; it may also inherit characteristics of its previous ancestors. This accounts for the well-known fact that if you save, say, antirrhinum seed from a pink-flowered plant, you do not necessarily get pink-flowered seedlings, but may have a variety of colours.

In the case of vegetative reproduction, some part of the old plant is cut away and induced to form roots, stems, flowers and leaves, and so become a complete plant on its own. This complete new plant will, in each case, be exactly similar to the plant from which it was taken, since no fusion of reproduction cells has occurred, and therefore no differences in characteristics have been induced. It does not matter whether the vegetative reproduction is effected by the use of a piece of root, a piece of stem, a leaf or a bud: in every case the new plant is like the plant from which it came.

A little consideration of these two kinds of reproduction will at once suggest to the gardener their particular values. Where vegetative reproduction can be simply and easily carried out, it is obvious that the amateur gardener will be glad to adopt this method, since by vegetative reproduction he can be sure of uniformity in his new plants. Its value to the commercial grower is also obvious, for plants of certain colours and forms can be given names, and sold under those names with the guarantee that they will behave as desired when grown in a customer's garden.

On the other hand, reproduction by seed is easy, seed is much easier to convey from one place to another than are cuttings or plants, and the number of seeds that a single plant will produce is, in most cases, far greater than the number of cuttings. Consequently, for certain classes of plants, seed-raising is definitely easier and better suited to the needs of the gardener, while seed-raising, as has already been hinted, is the method that is adopted by the hybridist, or raiser of new varieties of plants.

SEED-RAISING

Seed-raising will be again referred to in other chapters, but the general principles that have to be considered may be dealt with here. Seeds in Nature's garden leave the plants in a variety of ways, and are usually sown almost at once. One way of distribution is by the wind, as when dandelion and thistle seeds are blown through the air to alight on some distant patch of soil. Animals brush against other seeds and carry them on their coats to other parts of a field or wood. Birds and other animals eat certain seeds: these pass through the animal, and are left in the dung and guano, to develop later as the rains wash them down into the soil. Some seeds are thrown, by mechanical action of the drying seed-pods, to some distance from the parent plant. In all cases the seeds are distributed as soon as they are ripe enough, and this is a guide to the gardener as to the best time to sow seeds.

It is not, however, always convenient to sow seeds immediately they are ripe. Moreover, a good number of the seedlings might, in many cases, be injured by frosts if they were sown at the harvest season. Seeds that germinate at the turn of the year, and grow as the weather improves, are more likely to succeed; everyone must notice how well the spring seedlings grow in meadow and hedgerow. From this the gardener learns that seeds need, for good germination, warmth and (usually) gradually increasing light and adequate moisture.

SEEDS OUTDOORS

Seeds sown out in the open garden generally get enough moisture, but they are helped by the gardener in this respect. They are, first of all, sown on well-dug soil that lifts moisture from a considerable depth by capillary attraction, and they are also covered by a thin film of soil, which again assists them to remain moist. Whether a seed-bed is prepared specially, and seedlings raised there for transplanting, or whether seed is sown where it is to grow, these points should be observed:—

1. The bed should be so prepared that the surface is left fine, stone-free and reasonably fertile. A light dusting of fertiliser over the seed-bed a few days before sowing often makes all the difference between failure and success.

2. The seeds should be only lightly covered with soil. It requires some activity on the part of a developing seedling to move a soil layer sufficiently to allow the young leaf to come through, and a heavy soil layer may prevent this action.

3. The fine soil that covers the seed should come into close contact with the seed. The reason for this is that the first step in germination is the mechanical action of water being soaked up by the seed, in sufficient quantity to cause the seed to burst its outer covering. If the seeds lie in loose soil, some will absorb moisture more rapidly than others, and germination will be uneven.

4. The seed should only be sown at a season when moisture and warmth are likely to be available to the young plant. If these are not likely to be available in the open garden, some method of pro-

tection for the young plants must be devised—*i.e.*, cloches, frames, or glasshouses. (See below.)

Flower-seeds are often sown in the open garden where they are to mature: annuals, in particular, are grown in this way. Annuals are those plants that normally complete the whole life-cycle—germination, growth, flowering and fruiting—in one season. Biennials—*i.e.*, plants that take two seasons to complete their life-cycle—and perennials—plants that live on for an indefinite number of years—are also raised from seed; but in these cases it is more usual to sow the seed in prepared seed-beds, and to transplant the partly grown plants to their permanent positions later.

Vegetables are largely grown from seed, and usually in parallel lines on a special vegetable plot. (See Chapter XI.)

Rock-plants, shrubs and trees are generally raised (if from seed) in special pans or pots under glass, though certain of them can be sown in the open garden. Slow-growing plants, and plants that, like the majority of rockery subjects, are very small when they are young, are more conveniently managed in pots and pans.

SOWING UNDER GLASS

Sowing under glass differs from sowing in the open garden in that it can be done more or less all the year round, though the last two months of the year are not good months for seed-raising even in a greenhouse. In sowing under glass the points to keep in mind are these:—

1. Soil preparation must be designed to produce *the equivalent* of a well-drained soil below and friable, stone-free soil at the surface. The usual method is to give adequate drainage, with crocks over the hole

PLANTING-OUT SEEDLINGS

When sifting leaves, peat or soil, use the rough material for lining the bottom of seed boxes.

Plant out when the seedlings are large enough to handle; make them very firm in the soil.

Transplant Primula seedling with a trowel and see that a good ball of soil is attached to each root.

Fig. 43.

if a pot or pottery pan is used, or with not too well-fitting sides if a box of soil is used. Moisture is ensured by the use of peat-moss (or occasionally leaves) as a bottom layer, but an excess of moisture will be liable to cause " damping off," a disease that is deadly among seedlings. Sterilisation of the soil before use will help to avoid damping-off, but it is preferable that sterilisation of the various ingredients of the potting-soil should be done separately. Good soil mixture for potting is as follows: one part peat moss, one part sharp sand, two parts good garden loam.

2. Atmospheric conditions must be regulated so that the germinating seeds obtain fresh air, warmth and moisture. Darkness at first is desirable in most cases.

3. When seedlings have germinated, the maximum light possible, without scorching (adequate ventilation prevents this), is required, otherwise the seedlings become " drawn "—*i.e.*, they attempt to grow up into more light, and in so doing they lengthen too rapidly and become weakened.

OVERCROWDING

A trouble that affects seedlings in the open and under glass is caused by overcrowding, and if a batch of seedlings ever become weakened through this condition, they never fully recover. It is of the utmost importance that seedlings should be thinned out (*i.e.*, the unwanted seedlings carefully drawn out to leave the others more room) or pricked out (*i.e.*, lifted from the seed-box or bed and carefully planted out separately) as soon as they have made their second pair of leaves.

The use of carefully prepared potting-soil helps the gardener to effect this thinning and pricking out without damage to roots or stems—a very important point, as slight damage in the process of pricking out is responsible for a variety of plant ills.

TEMPERATURES

The temperatures needed for seed-raising vary chiefly according to the natural habitat of the wild plants from which our garden beauties have been developed. Consequently no particular temperature can be quoted as the right one, and each plant must be treated according to its special needs.

The natural habitat of a plant must, as a matter of fact, be a guide to successful cultivation all through its life. For example, the celery which we grow in our gardens has been developed from a plant that grows wild in marshy land. This is the key to its culture: it requires plenty of moisture, and for that reason the usual practice is to grow it in trenches, which can be easily flooded when rains are scarce. Plenty of decaying organic manure is also provided, for that also holds moisture for the plants. A good gardener studies the history of the plants he cultivates, and may often learn from historical facts how to get better results from his garden work.

HOW NEW PLANTS ARE RAISED

We have already said that new plants must be raised from seed, since all other methods of increasing plants result in plants of identical characteristics with the parent plant. Let us now describe the various stages by which the hybridist obtains the kind of new plant he wants.

Seedling plants will, as stated, have some of the characteristics of each parent—the mother plant on which the seed grew, and the father plant which provided the fertilising pollen. Hybridists therefore begin by selecting two plants, one to become the mother plant, and the other the father plant.

For the benefit of those who have no knowledge of botany, a few facts concerning the structure of plants may be mentioned here. Most flowering plants have, in addition to coloured sepals, bracts or petals, both female and male organs. The female organs are the ovaries, which will later, if fertilised, develop into the seed-pods or fruits. The ovaries are generally at the base of the pistil, which is often a tubular stem, on the tip of which is (at the time when the flower is ready for fertilisation) a sticky fluid. The male organs are the stamens, which hold sacs of pollen. When these sacs are "ripe" they open, revealing pollen dust—the dust which is carried by insects or other agencies to the sticky head of a pistil, thus effecting fertilisation.

If the flowers are left to grow naturally, the pistil may receive fertilising dust from any unknown plant that has been visited by insects, or it may, in some cases, receive the fertilising dust from stamens in the same flower, or from a flower on the same plant. The hybridist does not want either of these to happen, so he begins by removing from the chosen mother plant all the stamens, before the pollen dust is ripe. This prevents self-pollination. It may be noted here that certain flowers—the begonia, for instance—have male and female organs on separate flowers, but the majority of flowers have both male and female in one flower.

The hybridist then makes other undesirable pollination impossible by protecting the mother flower: a covering of muslin is a common way to protect it. Next he waits until, by the sticky surface of the pistil head, he knows that the flower is ready to be fertilised, and then he carries from the chosen father plant some ripe pollen dust, and places it on the pistil of the mother plant. Again the muslin or other protection is put in place, and it is only removed when it is seen that the seeds are developing.

These seeds are carefully harvested, and a record of the " cross ", stating the variety of mother and father plants, is kept. The seeds are in due course sown, and the resulting seedlings are a " hybrid " or " cross " between the two varieties.

This by no means ends the work of the hybridist: often the first generation of seedlings is apparently worthless, when the flowers come; but if these are again crossed one with another, surprising results may occur. Hybridists work on one strain for many years before it becomes marketable, and often a great deal of their work turns out to be of little apparent value. Then again, in the case of roses and similar plants, a cross may be made quite easily, but it would mean a long wait if the seedlings were grown on in the usual way, so hybridising is often followed up by budding or grafting, in order to get a plant that will flower or fruit in a year or two. When annuals are raised by the hybridist, and a good-quality flower or vegetable secured, there must still be a good many years of patient work, raising seedlings, and weeding out " rogues "—*i.e.*, seedlings that revert to other characteristics, instead of growing as desired. By such means the strain is gradually purified until it is sufficiently stabilised to be put on the market. A strain of seeds of poor quality, in which " rogues " are still plentiful, will ruin a seedsman's reputation.

Hybridising is, however, a fascinating hobby or life occupation, and well worth studying in more detail by those who can afford the time it demands.

VEGETATIVE REPRODUCTION

Now let us turn to the other method of increasing plants—vegetative reproduction. As already stated, many different parts of a plant have this power of developing into complete new plants if severed from the parent plant. All that is required, apparently, is that the gardener should, by some means, keep the severed portion in normal healthy condition while it is an in-

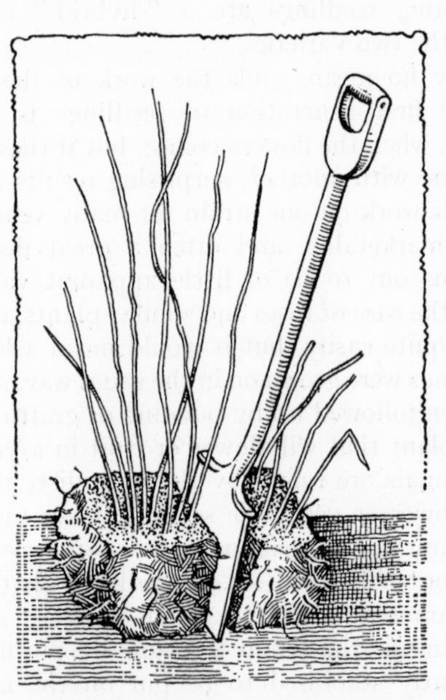

FIG. 44.—Division of large roots by a spade, or merely take off pieces with a sharp knife, allowing some stems and some roots to each portion. Avoid replanting diseased roots.

complete plant, and so allow it to develop. If it cannot be kept normally healthy it will, of course, die.

Root Division is perhaps the simplest form of vegetative reproduction. In this, a part of the plant is severed "vertically", as it were—*i.e.*, a piece is broken away—

and this piece will be composed of some leaf and stem, and some root. If it is replanted quickly, before it dries out, such a severed portion will nearly always live on and grow to a good size. Herbaceous plants—plants that live on for several seasons, but die down almost to the ground in winter—are generally increased in this way. In the case of plants that spread rapidly through the soil, the newer outside portions of an old clump are generally the best parts, and the gardener who renovates the herbaceous border every two or three years will retain just enough of these outer portions to replant his border, and will discard the rest.

Root Cuttings. Some plants do not divide very easily in this manner. They may have different kinds of roots: fleshy roots, such as delphinium and oriental poppy roots, or deep tap roots, such as those of the lupin. In the case of fleshy roots, an easy method of increase is by root-cuttings. When growth is inactive, at the end of the season, the plant is lifted, and the fleshy roots can be cut into pieces of the length and size of a man's first finger. It is usual to cut straight across the top, and slanting across the bottom, as this is a guide when replanting. The portions of root are generally planted out in a nursery bed, the tops being about an inch below the soil surface, and the root-cuttings set upright, in well-drained, sandy soil. They rarely fail to develop into good plants for setting out later in the border.

Sometimes, as in the case of peonies, it is best not to disturb the old plant, but to draw the soil away from the roots on one side, and take off carefully a portion of the root, together with a " crown " or growing point. This is then replanted, the crown being set an inch below the surface.

If neither root cuttings nor root division seem practicable, cuttings of top growth are made.

Stem Cuttings are of two kinds: soft cuttings—that is, of soft growth still actively developing—and woody cuttings, or cuttings of dormant woody growth, preferably growth of not more than one season, but sufficiently far developed not to be still sappy and green.

FIG. 45.—Stem cuttings.

The most likely place for roots to develop on a stem is at the leaf-joint, and in making either soft or hard cuttings the general rule is to cut the stem across just below the leaf-joint. There are a few exceptions to this rule, like clematis and salix, but they will be found by experience.

Leaves left on the part of the cutting that will go

under the soil would decay, and might set up the sort of unhealthy soil conditions that would prove fatal, so such leaves are always cut away. In some cases—*e.g.*, with gooseberries—dormant buds on the middle part of the cutting are rubbed away, since the desire of the cultivator is to have a plant on a single stem at the base, and too many buds might develop into stems and make a low, feathered bush. If cuttings of woody stems are made, and the top part of the growth is rather too soft and sappy, this also is sometimes removed with advantage. The " made " woody cutting is usually a stem of which half will go into the ground, while on the half that is left above ground there are five or six good dormant leaf-buds, and no soft, sappy tip. A " made " soft cutting should usually have about four or five pairs of leaves above the ground, and enough stripped stem to hold the cutting firm in the soil.

Several substances, like Hortomone A or Seradix A, are sold by sundries-men for use in preparing cuttings. The base of the cuttings is steeped in solution for a few hours before the cuttings are inserted, and root formation is thereby speeded up remarkably. Instructions are given with each type of chemical. In any case, where ordinary cuttings have failed, treated cuttings should certainly be tried.

Soil for rooting cuttings must be of good quality, but very open and sandy. Cuttings can be rooted in pure sand or in vermiculite, but the plants must be potted up in better soil when the roots have formed, or they will be starved. If the soil used for cuttings is not sandy and open, the chances are that the stems will be too moist, and, having little air and too much moisture, they will decay, instead of remaining healthy and forming roots. Hard-wooded cuttings root quite easily during the dormant season out of doors, or without special care. Soft cuttings, taken during the active growing season, need more preparation. They have leaf-surfaces that are giving off moisture all the time, and unless this can be prevented, until the roots form, the cuttings will wither and die. For this reason, soft cuttings are generally rooted in frames or under cloches. This keeps the air

FIG. 46.—Cuttings are potted in spring into 3-in. pots. The soil is made firm around the roots with a blunt stick.

stationary round the plants, and spraying overhead once or twice daily helps to prevent evaporation.

A cutting-frame need not be an elaborate structure: it must hold sandy soil or pure sand, it must be partially shaded (sun causes excessive evaporation), and it must keep stationary air round the plants. A hole in the border, a foot deep, with sandy soil in the bottom and a sheet of glass over it, makes a good frame, which can be shaded with brushwood or newspaper, as desirable.

Cuttings are inserted fairly close together, and watered overhead; then for a time they remain unattended, except that the glass is wiped daily, so that moisture does not drip constantly from it on to the plants. As soon as fresh growth is visible on the cuttings it can be assumed that roots have formed, and gradually more air and light can be allowed. Soft cuttings taken in summer in the open garden root very readily with improvised

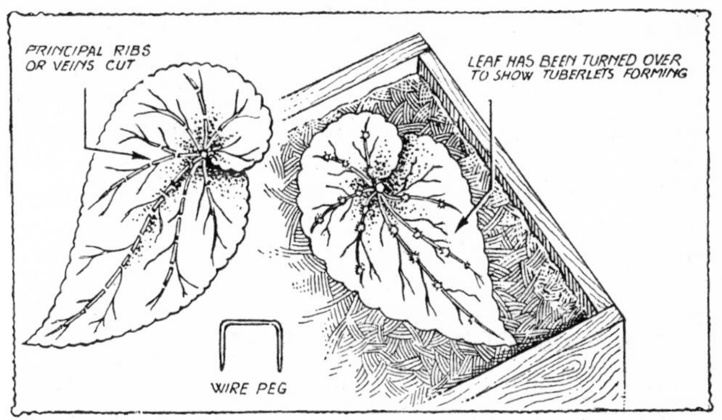

FIG. 47—Leaf cuttings; a begonia leaf after being pegged down on to moist sandy soil. Note the formation of tuberlets on the underside.

shelter of this kind, or soft cuttings can be taken at any time in a propagating frame in a glasshouse. Special propagating frames are on sale: they are designed to fulfil the requirements of cuttings with ease of manipulation.

Leaf Cuttings are another way to increase plants. They are treated on exactly the same principles as soft stem cuttings. A begonia rex leaf, for instance, is laid right side up on a pan of moist sand or sandy loam, after the veins on the underside have been cut across in several places. Roots form at the veins, and the leaf is then cut into portions, each having its roots, and thenceforward each is treated as a separate plant.

Layers are a method of taking cuttings, but allowing the new plant to continue to draw on the food supplies of the old plant while it is making its own roots. A part of the stem of the old plant is bent down to the soil, and pegged down so that it passes under the surface. The protruding tip is staked, as a rule, except in the case of small plants such as carnations, and the part of the stem below the soil is " notched " or cut partly through with a slanting upward cut, before it is bent down, so that an open " tongue " is under the soil. Roots form at this cut, while the tip or " layer " is still able to draw on the parent for food. Later the stem that links the two is cut through, and the layer becomes a complete new plant on its own. Many plants that are difficult to root from ordinary cuttings can be increased by layering.

BUDDING AND GRAFTING

Budding and grafting are the same process, the difference being only in the size of the transaction. Both are a means of obtaining plants of certain named varieties quickly, without waiting for the new plants to grow their own roots and become established. In some cases they are practised, too, in order to get greater vigour into the plant that is desired.

In budding or grafting, a well-rooted plant of wild type, or of some unwanted variety, is used as the " stock ". On to this is budded or grafted a piece of a plant that the gardener wishes to possess, in such a way that this new piece grows, taking its food supplies through the root system of the inferior, or unwanted variety. In due course all the top growth of the old stock is cut away, leaving only the budded or grafted portion to develop: the stock is thus to all intents and purposes changed to some new variety. The bud or graft is called the " scion ".

Budding is perhaps the easier operation. To bud a rose on to a briar, or a fruiting or flowering cherry on to a wild cherry, follow these instructions carefully:—

1. In June or July (budding time) have ready the stock. If a bush rose is desired, any shaped wild briar is satisfactory, as the bud will be inserted in the main stem immediately below the soil surface. If a standard is wanted, the stock must have been grown to the desired height for the head. It speeds up the formation of a head if a briar that has been previously headed back can be used—*i.e.*, a stock that has already a single straight stem, with branches at the desired height. A bud can then be inserted on the upper side of each of the side branches, near the main stem, and the head will be formed as the buds grow.
2. Raffia and a budding knife or penknife are required.
3. Buds for budding are dormant leaf-buds: those on the lower part of a stem that has carried a flower are suitable, as they will be well developed.
4. Keep the buds fresh until required. If a stem is taken from the rose that is to give the scion or bud, keep it in water until the budding is done.
5. Prepare the bud by making an arc-like cut behind the bud so that it comes away with an oval piece of bark round it. There will also be a small woody part of the stem behind the bud. Remove this carefully, without damaging the bud. If a bud is damaged, discard it and use another. Cut away the leaf that is at the joint where the bud is,

but leave a tiny portion of the stalk, as this can be used in handling the bud.

6. Prepare the stock by making a T-shaped cut in the bark, where the bud is wanted. Any place on the stem can be chosen, provided the bark there is in the half-ripe condition that allows it to be lifted easily with the blunt end of the budding knife. Lift the two corners of bark, and carefully insert the bud, laying the bark round the bud close against the inner wood of the stock. Lay back the cut points of bark, over the bark of the scion, leaving the bud itself pointing outward. Bind with raffia, covering the cut edges of bark, but allowing the bud to protrude.

All being well, the bud will, in the course of a week or two, swell up and look plump and healthy. The raffia binding can then be loosened if desired, but it should remain in position, as it helps the healing of the wound.

If the budding operation is a failure, the bud will wither, and probably drop away from the stock; budding will in this case have to be repeated on some other part of the stem.

Do not, in any case, cut back the stock until the following spring. When the bud begins to grow, however, all parts of the stock above the bud must be cut away, leaving only the new bud (or buds) to develop.

Grafting is precisely the same operation as budding, with the single difference that in grafting a larger portion of "scion" is used. Grafting is generally done in late winter or early spring, when the sap is beginning to rise in the stock. (It may be remarked that in most garden operations those dealing with soft growth are carried out in summer, and those dealing with hard, woody growth are carried out in winter.)

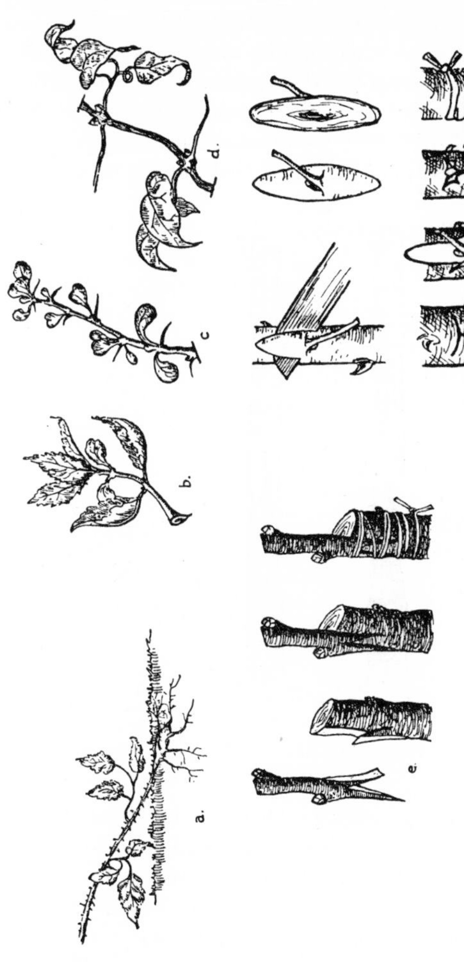

FIG. 48.—Raising new plants.

(a) Loganberry shoot layered into the soil.
(b) Cutting of dahlia with heel of old wood attached.
(c) Nodal cutting of barberry.
(d) Inter-nodal cutting of clematis.
(e) Method of tongue-grafting, showing preparation of scion and stock, and tying the graft with raffia; afterwards grafting-wax is fixed.
(f) Method of budding a rose, and preparation of bud ready for insertion into the briar stock. When tied with raffia, the bud just peeps out of the raffia.

An important point in grafting is to make sure that the scion is not further advanced in growth than is the stock: if it is, the scion will not be able quickly to draw on the feeding system of the stock, and failure will result. A precaution is to cut from the plants that produce the scions sufficient dormant stems for the purpose, in January, and heel them in, or lay them under moist soil

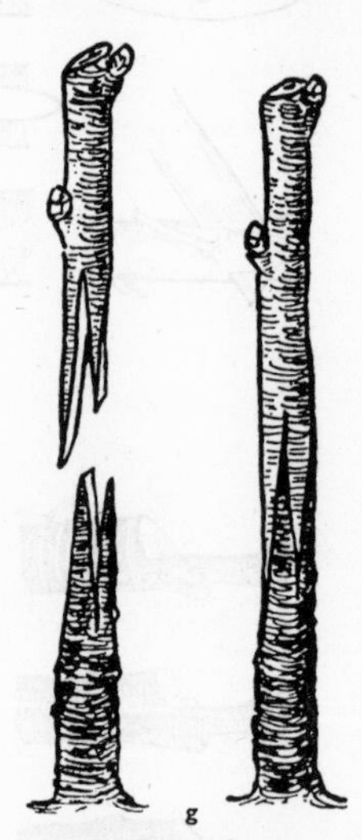

FIG. 48A.

(g) Method of tongue-grafting a young cherry stock with a prepared scion.

in a cool place for a couple of months. The buds remain dormant; the roots of the stock are, meanwhile, actively feeding, and the sap is rising, so that when, in April, the graft is made, there is a good chance of success.

In grafting, the "scion" is not a bud, but a piece of the stem, carrying several dormant buds. It should be a sound, ripe piece of one-year-old wood. It can be cut wedge-shaped at the base; or slanting, with a long strip of bark left attached, this to be bound in position across the cut stem of the stock, and down the side, making the union extra sure; or the cuts can be made in any convenient way, so long as the parts of the scion and stock immediately under the bark are allowed to meet, for it is at this point that effective union can take place.

Grafts are placed in position—sometimes several grafts round the edges of a trunk—in the most convenient way, and at the height desired. The stock has sometimes to be sawn off to take the grafts; but it is also possible to insert grafts in the side of the stem, just as buds are inserted. In all cases the principle is the same: the cambium layers, immediately beneath the bark, must meet.

Sometimes—nearly always, in fact—supports are needed to keep the grafts in position. Grafting-wax is used to keep out rain and help to stabilise the grafts, and raffia, etc., are used for binding. The exact method of grafting must vary according to size of stock and scion, etc. If they are of the same size, saddle grafting—*i.e.*, two inverted V-cuts that correspond on both stock and scion—are made, and the two pieces just bound together. A glance at the illustrations will serve to show the principles of grafting in practice.

Not only can wild trees be grafted: old, unfruitful trees, or trees that are of old inferior varieties, can often be brought quickly into good, profitable trees by being cut back and grafted again, and the task is so fascinating that every gardener ought to try his hand.

CHAPTER IX

FLOWERS FOR GARDEN AND HOME DECORATION; LAWNS AND CARE OF LAWNS

GARDENERS classify flowering plants rather differently from the usual botanical classification, because gardeners are concerned with practical methods of cultivation. Gardeners divide them roughly into two groups: those that grow from seed, flower once, fruit, and then die, to be succeeded by another generation that comes from the ripe seeds; and those plants that begin in the same way, but can go on producing crops of flowers and fruits for an indefinite number of years.

These two main groups are again divided: the first is divided into those plants that complete the whole life-cycle in one season and those that may take two (or sometimes even three) seasons to reach the flowering stage, but are exhausted after one burst of flowering. The plants that grow and die in one season are called annuals. Those that take normally two seasons are called biennials. These again are divided according to their hardiness—that is, whether they are able to stand our normal winters without special protection or heat, or whether they must be wintered, or started in early spring, in a frame or glasshouse.

The second large group of flowering plants is also divided into secondary groups: there are plants that live on for many years, but of which the flower-stems and top growth generally die down every season; there are also plants that live on year after year, retaining the stem-growth that they made the previous season, and gradually developing a woody structure. This second

FLOWERS FOR SPRING

Primrose. Iris.

Narcissus naturalised in grass.

Lupin: Russell Hybrids.

Bush Roses are at their best in June.

LATE AUTUMN

Dahlias.

Colchicum.

WINTER

Witch Hazel: Hamamelis.

Snowdrops.

group includes all shrubs, trees, roses, orchard fruits and hedge-plants.

Again, in these groups there are some plants that stand our normal winters in the open, and some that must be protected—*i.e.*, some hardy and some tender.

So we have for garden decoration the following groups of flowering or ornamental plants:—

Hardy annuals, sown each spring to flower the same year.

Half-hardy annuals, sown each spring, but generally raised under glass, because they would die if exposed to frost.

Hardy biennials, sown in spring, to flower in the second year.

Half-hardy biennials, like the hardy biennials, but grown during winter under glass.

Hardy herbaceous plants, that live for many years, but die back to ground-level each winter.

Half-hardy herbaceous perennials, generally spoken of as bedding plants, grown on from year to year, but always lifted from the open garden and wintered under glass or (if they have tuberous roots) stored in a dormant state.

Hardy shrubs and trees. Grown on for many seasons outdoors.

Half-hardy shrubs. This is a class that is often used for bedding. The shrubby calceolaria, for instance, and the common bedding geranium would, if allowed to grow on in congenial surroundings, become woody shrubs, but since they are not suited to our climate, we usually propagate afresh from cuttings each season, and use only young plants, not woody, for garden decoration.

There are, in addition, plants of all classes that the greenhouse owner can grow for greenhouse decoration and that are unsuitable for growing outdoors at any

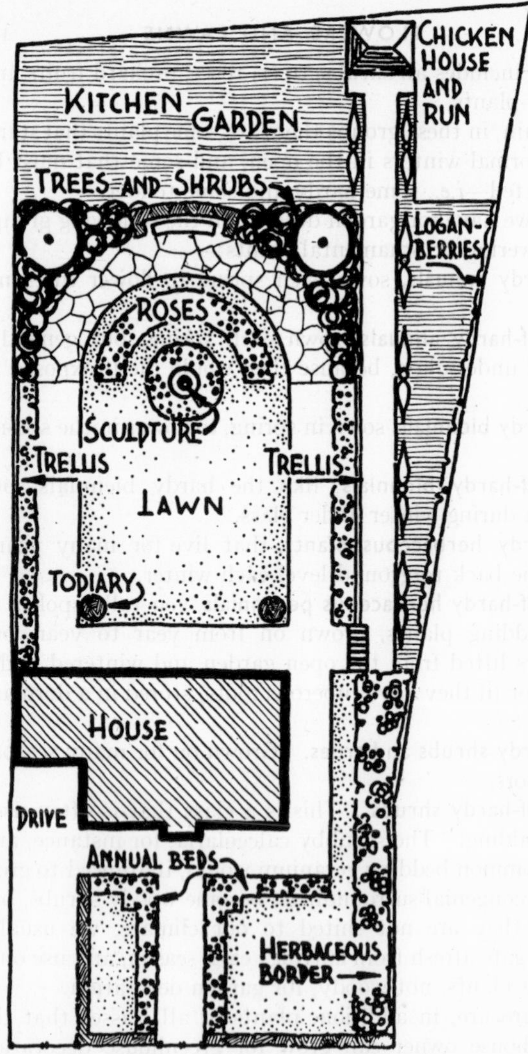

FIG. 49.—Layout of flower garden.

Provision is made for all types of flowers, and the kitchen-garden, chicken-run and fruit are placed at the end and in the corner of the garden.

season: greenhouse annuals, greenhouse biennials, greenhouse herbaceous plants, greenhouse shrubs, etc.

All plants that live on over a number of years are called perennials, and in this group are included bulbs, shrubs, and herbaceous plants.

Let us take each class of flowering plant in turn, and see how and why it should be used in garden decoration.

ANNUALS

Hardy annuals are the easiest of all garden flowers. This class includes the common orange marigold, blue love in a mist, white sweet alyssum, scarlet flax, pink clarkia, and gold or chocolate calliopsis, among many others. It will at once be seen that a garden could be made bright and gay through the summer with the use of annuals alone. As a matter of fact, in a large garden it is generally thought best to use annuals in special beds and borders turned over entirely to them for the season. This is because annuals all need more or less the same soil preparation and the same cultural treatment, and it is easy to dig in winter or early spring, sow, thin and hoe, and finally clear away the faded, withered plants all at the same time. A border of annuals, so arranged that the taller annuals grow mostly to the back, while broad-spreading groups of dwarf annuals occupy the front edge of the border, makes a very fine display for some weeks towards the end of the summer.

To grow annuals in this way the border should be prepared by deep digging, adding bonemeal (2 to 4 oz. per square yard) during digging. This will encourage flower production. About March or April the soil surface will be raked to a fine, even tilth, and the annual seeds of perfectly hardy nature can be sown first, while more tender types can be sown later, or raised under glass and planted out in May.

Broadcast sowing—scattering the seed thinly over the prescribed patch of soil—is best for this type of border, as formality is undesirable. Seedlings must never overcrowd: they can be thinned out as they grow, each plant being allowed all the room it wants, so that it never jostles its neighbour. In this way fine, symmetrical, bushy plants will be developed that will carry numerous good flowers. Some annuals are better if the central growing tip of the stem is pinched out early, to encourage a number of side growths to come from the lower part of the stem: this makes an extra bushy plant, but in certain cases it delays the appearance of flowers so much that it is not wise to "stop" it in this way.

A few dwarf annuals—Virginian stock, night-scented stock and flax are examples—can be sown rather thinly as edgings, and then left alone, with no thinning of the seedlings.

Some of the tall, showy annuals require a little support, particularly when grown in windy places. A few twigs pushed in among the tiny seedlings, so that the tender growths come up among the twigs, make an effective support for Shirley poppies and similar flowers. Regular attention to thinning will in many cases obviate the need for supports, as well-grown plants are better able to stand alone than plants that have become weedy and drawn through crowding.

Half-hardy annuals are grown where they are sown in some cases, particularly those which are difficult to transplant satisfactorily. A great many are raised in frames and glasshouses. For this all that is required is sufficient protection to keep out frosts, while admitting sunlight and air. Many a gardener has raised his half-hardy annuals on a kitchen window-ledge, or in an attic under a skylight. Seed-boxes are generally filled at the bottom with some material to prevent the soil being washed through the ill-fitting sides. Old leaves or peat-moss litter can be used for the purpose. Good potting-soil (half loam, quarter sand and quarter leaf-mould or peat moss, all sieved and well mixed) should be filled loosely into the box, to the rim, and then pressed down flat with a wooden presser or cement trowel. This leaves the compost a little below the rim. Seeds can be sown in lines thinly, or broadcast over the box, and covered with a fine dusting of soil.

Seed-boxes are best watered by partial immersion; if this is not practicable, water with a fine syringe, to avoid disturbing the seeds. Cover each box with a sheet of paper at first, to exclude the light and help to retain surface moisture, but immediately germination has taken place remove the paper and stand the box as near the glass as possible. Give plenty of air on all occasions when the weather permits, and avoid scorching, or allowing the plants to become drawn through lack of sunlight.

When seedlings have made a second pair of leaves (true leaves, the gardener calls them, as the first leaves are those that came from the seed, and are usually quite unlike the other leaves of a plant), it is time to prick out. A tool for pricking out is an ordinary plant label, with a wedge-shaped piece cut out at one end. In this cleft stick the seedling can be lifted from the seed-bed or box without actual handling, and can be transferred to a hole made for it previously by the same stick. Soil can then be levered against the neck of the seedling to make it firm.

Annuals are usually pricked out into other boxes, similar to the seed-box, and set 3 or 4 inches apart, according to their kind. These boxes are the sort offered in May for bedding out: the seedlings (a certain number go to a box) have just about enough room in them to develop to a nice size for bedding, and a box of healthy bedding plants should be well filled with bushy, short growth. If a gardener buys his bedding plants, he should reject any that appear spindly and weak, for they will never recover, however carefully they are nursed later.

BIENNIALS

Canterbury bells are a typical example of garden biennials. Seed of these is usually sown in lines across a prepared plot of ground in the open garden. The lines should be at least 8 inches apart at sowing time, to allow for the use of the hoe. When the seedlings are well up, some can be taken out and transplanted to other rows, leaving the plants about 6 inches apart in the rows, to grow on thus until the late autumn, when they can be moved to their flowering quarters. They should have made good, leafy plants by the autumn, and in the spring each should throw up a good flowering stem. In the case of Canterbury bells it sometimes happens that the plants are not well enough developed by May or June to send up a flowering stem, and the strange thing is that these plants will not flower later in the same year, but will, in this case, wait another season. Plants that flower in the third spring often send up several flowering stems instead of one.

Wallflowers and forget-me-nots are typical of flowers that we usually call biennials, and grow in this same way; but if left to grow on, these plants would often live for several seasons. They are therefore truly perennial in nature, but for gardening purposes they are classed as biennials, because biennial treatment gives the best results.

Tender biennials can only be grown by those who can use the greenhouse in winter. Certain stocks are frequently grown from summer sowings, to flower early the next season, and so are varieties of the carnation and pink family. Treatment is similar to ordinary biennial treatment, except that protection of some kind (sometimes just cloches in the open) is given during the cold weather.

The use of both classes of biennials in the garden is mainly to provide masses of early flower, since biennials mostly flower in early summer, when other flowers are comparatively scarce.

HERBACEOUS PERENNIALS

Everyone knows something of the herbaceous border. This is generally the pride of the large garden owner. In it grow on from season to season the perennial plants of herbaceous character, dying back for the most part in winter, and reappearing in full force when the sunnier days come again. A good herbaceous border should have something of interest in it from early spring to late autumn, and, if possible, even the winter should bring its share of beauty to the picture. There are such plants as the winter-flowering anemones, primulas, Christmas roses, and the earliest of the bulbs—winter aconites and snowdrops—that grace the fine days of December and January, and a good planting scheme for the border will include these.

A glance at a plan of a herbaceous border will show the principles on which it is designed. First there must be beauty of colour and flower at all seasons. This must be well distributed along the border. Then there must be harmony in the colours, and a reasonable planning of outlines; tall groups here and there towards the back, and broad, open " bays " of dwarf flowers in the front of the border. Absolute uniformity along the border is never sought, but careful planning must allow those who walk the length of the border to find new pictures every few steps, and not to miss the beauty of any of the plants.

Herbaceous plants are planted either in autumn or spring. Autumn planting is best for most subjects, and most gardens, because this allows the roots to become established before top growth is demanded on the plants.

Prepare the soil by double digging—*i.e.*, breaking the subsoil and turning over the top—and manure it adequately before planting. Bonemeal as advised for annuals is useful, but a quantity of humus in some form (stable farm or compost manuring) is also advisable, since the plants will remain a long time without further attention. A label for each group of plants, set in place before any planting is done, assists in keeping to the prepared plan, and is a guide when hoeing the border later.

Plant firmly, spreading the roots out well, and seeing that the moist soil is pressed well down over them.

After initial planting, the treatment of an herbaceous border is this:—

1. Hoeing is done regularly as long as soil is visible between the plants.

2. Staking is done *before* the plants seem to need it. Stakes should be sufficient to allow for staking out, and a bunch of stems should never be *tied in* to a single stake, so that they crowd each other.

3. An occasional dose of general fertiliser given when the plants are beginning to throw up flower-stems will help amazingly.

4. After three years the plants are all lifted from the border, in autumn or spring, divided if necessary (as described in Chapter VIII), and replanted after the soil has been dug and manured. Certain plants, such as peonies, that resent disturbance need not be lifted, but all the ordinary perennials

of the Michaelmas daisy type must be lifted, and a good part them will have to be discarded or used for other borders, or they will get overcrowded and cease to bloom well. It is also necessary with this type of flower to thin out the flower-stems in the second and third years, as these become so numerous that the flowers suffer in quality. (*N.B.*—When these flowers are grown for Shows only one spike is allowed to each root, in order to get the best flowers and a shapely spray. Single stems of this kind actually make a better show of colour in a border than do several less well grown stems.)

Tender Plants. In the small garden borders are not often so strictly classified: they are generally mixed borders—that is, they may have annuals, perennials and biennials in them, and even some shrubs. In addition, they may have a number of the tender or half-hardy perennials, such as the blue salvia used for bedding purposes. In such cases the tender plants are lifted at the end of the summer, and wintered in a glasshouse, or frame.

The common practice with gardeners is to pack as many plants as possible into winter quarters, and for this reason they often take cuttings at the end of summer, and insert these close together in boxes. The boxes can be wintered economically, and will provide sufficient new plants for re-stocking beds and borders another season. The old plants which have exhausted themselves by flowering all summer are consigned to the scrap-heap. This happens with bedding geraniums, calceolarias, and so on. The glasshouse or frame used for wintering these needs only to be kept to about 40 degrees (F.), so that frost is excluded, and the plants are not over-watered during the cold weather, so that they do not make a lot of growth until the spring. In the following summer, however, they grow quickly to flowering condition, and so the process is repeated, each season.

Bulbs are among the herbaceous perennials, but they are a distinct type of plant. In the bulb the leaves made during the growing season seem to "telescope downwards" into the fleshy scales of the bulb. Thus the bulb is a storehouse of plant-food. This makes bulbs a very easy subject for the gardener, so long as bulbs can be bought. He has only to plant them, to be pretty sure of good flowers, for they have already their food in them, and do not depend on the quality of the soil. What is important, however, is that bulbs should be put into soil that is not waterlogged, for a bulb that rests in a small puddle of stagnant water will decay instead of growing. The general rule with bulbs, therefore, is to plant each with a small handful of sharp sand below the base. Set out in this way, bulbs rarely fail. As to depth, the rule is that twice the depth of the bulb itself should be the depth of soil covering it. In sandy soil bulbs can be set even deeper.

Tender bulbs—that is, bulbs that may be damaged by frost if left in the ground—are often used for summer flowering. Gladiolas are an example. In such cases the bulbs are lifted when the foliage begins to turn colour in autumn, dried a little, cleaned, and stored in a shed away from frost, to be replanted in the spring.

Bulbs of many kinds can be used in many parts of the garden. There are small bulbs suitable for growing in the soil-pockets of a rock garden. There are bulbs specially suitable for growing in woodland walks. There are bulbs specially suited for growing in grass under trees, such as under the orchard fruit trees. In addition, bulbs can be very useful in groups in the mixed border.

A good principle to adopt is always to set bulbs in groups of six, and plants (with few exceptions) in groups of not less than three, for grouping in this manner gives the showiest results.

Roses and other Shrubs. There is no strict line of demarcation between shrubs and trees. Both are plants that retain their stems season after season, become gradually woody, and add each year to their stature. A rough distinction is, however, made between plants that are grown as bushes or are of low stature, and plants that grow to immense heights. What we call a tree is usually a woody-stemmed plant growing with a single stem at the base, while woody-stemmed plants that have several branches coming from the ground-level are usually called shrubs. As before stated, however, the line of demarcation between the two classes scarcely exists.

In the flower-garden roses are the most common flowering shrubs grown, and they are easily the showiest and most useful of shrubs to the small garden owner. They are also the ideal plants for a busy week-end gardener, for they do not need much attention, except once or twice a year, when pruning has to be done. At other times spraying to keep down pests or disease, and the removal of dead flowers and broken stems, are all the gardener need trouble about. An occasional dressing with fertiliser keeps the roses in good condition, and no lifting and dividing, re-sowing or re-planting are required.

Preparation for rose-planting is similar to the preparation for all other garden shrubs (except that lime-haters need no lime), and can be briefly described. The ground should be double dug, in the case of rose-beds, or, for single specimen roses and climbers against walls or pergolas, holes at least 2 feet deep should be opened. Whether the soil is stiff, greasy clay or pure sand, the aim of the gardener is to bring it into the condition we describe as a "medium loam"—that is, neither extreme, but an open, friable loam that will hold both air and moisture. The addition of good compost material to either extreme of soil will improve its texture. Chalk added to sandy soils and lime and grit added to greasy clay will also help the roses. Bonemeal added to any kind of soil will encourage flower production.

In planting, provide a stake to each rose unless the roses have been pruned back to only a few inches high at planting time. The best time for planting is in autumn, but any time up to the middle of March will do. Late-planted roses are sometimes cut back by the nurseryman, and staking is then superfluous. Plant firmly, spreading out the roots, and shaking fine soil in among the finer roots; tread firmly each soil layer, so that all roots are in close contact with moist soil particles. Planting cannot be done when soil is water-logged, for obvious reasons, and it is also fatal to plant in frosty soil. Roses received from a nursery during a frosty period should be heeled into the ground in a protected corner of the garden, or laid in a shed and kept covered with damp soil or sacks until the weather improves.

Always remember to label roses at planting time, and follow this practice with any other trees and shrubs. Pruning of shrubs and trees varies with the variety, and if the name is missing, pruning may easily be wrongly done.

After-care of shrubs, including roses, can be summed up in two words—feeding, and pruning. An annual mulch of old decayed manure over the soil surface in spring, with dressings of bonemeal lightly hoed in during autumn for those shrubs that are wanted to flower, will keep most shrubs growing well. It is a mistake to use the digging-fork freely among shrubs: hoe off weeds and use surface mulches of manure or of good new soil instead of forking. Shrub-roots often lie very near the surface, and the plants suffer from too much root disturbance.

Pruning is the *pons asinorum* of the would-be gardener. Pruning cannot be dealt with in very great detail in a book of general reference, but if a gardener once understands the principles that underlie this garden task, he can be left to work out his own salvation in the shrubbery.

Pruning is the removal of unwanted parts of a shrub in order to:—

(*a*) improve its symmetry;

(*b*) encourage flower production;

(*c*) encourage development of *new* stems rather than old;

(*d*) maintain the general health of the whole plant;

(*e*) restrict the size of the plant to its limited position.

In order to achieve these objects the natural growth of each plant must be considered, and, in addition, the gardener must know what the effect of cuts made at different points will be. Let us take the last point first. If you cut off the top of a stem, the immediate reaction of the plant will be that the last bud, or perhaps the last three buds left on the shortened stem, will break out into new growth. These new stems will each be not quite so strong as the central stem was, and they will give to the plant a "feathered" or branched appearance. The longer the piece of central stem removed, the stronger and fewer such growths will result. If a stem is cut back to a point just above a bud that points outwards from the centre of the plant, the new stem that develops will point and grow outwards: the opposite is also true. Another point in this connexion is that the more wood you remove from a plant, the more new stem-growth will result, whereas light pruning will be followed not by stem-growth, but by the formation of flower-buds. In other words, light pruning leads to the formation of

FIG. 50.—To prune a bush rose, first cut out weak and worn out wood, then shorten the remaining stems as seen here. Prune back weak growers very hard, but leave more wood on the strong growers.

many flowers, hard pruning leads to greater strength in the new growths, less flowers, but often these flowers will be of larger size. Pruning that allows more light to reach the remaining stems will encourage flower-bud formation, however, so that judicious hard pruning may be as helpful as light pruning.

Now to apply this knowledge to the plants, according to their habit of growth. Some shrubs grow more or less naturally to the shape of " cordons "—that is, they keep a skeleton of radiating branches, along which form short " spurs " that carry the flowers and fruit each season. Cydonias do this, and so do many of the fruiting cherries. These shrubs need almost no pruning, unless their food supplies are ill-balanced, in which case it may be necessary to correct the tendency to make stems and leaves instead of flowers by dressing the soil with bone-meal, basic slag or superphosphate.

There are also times when shrubs of this kind can be encouraged to make the flowering spurs, by trimming back the side stems of one year's growth, leaving only a bud or two at the base of this new wood.

Again, there are shrubs that flower on comparatively new wood, either wood of the current season, or new wood that grew in the previous summer after the flowers had faded. Forsythia is a shrub that flowers on wood that grows after the flowers fade. You can treat it in one of two ways: either you can cut it back almost to the old wood every spring, after the flowers fade, which will result in very strong new stems that will have extra fine flowers on them, or you can leave it unpruned, or merely thin out the stems just enough to leave plenty to cover a pillar or fence. This last method results in a smother growth with masses of flowers, but the individual flowers are not so fine.

Buddleia variabilis is an example of a shrub that flowers on wood of the current season's growth. You get the best results with this if you cut it hard back in February, leaving only a few buds at the base of the last season's wood. Fresh, long stems result, and these, too, should be thinned out—that is, as soon as they are large enough to handle, nip off those you do not want. In this way the shrub will produce fine stems and magnificent panicles of flowers. (For further information *re* the use of shrubs and trees, see Chapter XV.)

PRUNING OF HEDGES

Floral and berrying hedges are pruned in the normal way for the variety and kind of shrub, always remembering that a degree of formality is inseparable from the hedge style of cultivation. *Berberis stenophylla*, for example, when grown as a specimen plant, is cut back hard immediately the flowers fade, and then fed well to encourage long, strong arching stems that will flower magnificently next season. When growing as a hedge, it is sometimes preferable to cut the stems back again in August, part way, the result being a more formal outline, with plenty of flower, but lacking the great beauty of the long, arching stem that is so desirable in a specimen. Where space permits, an established hedge can be cut back once only, as are specimen plants.

Formal hedges of non-flowering type are treated according to their constitution. Conifer hedges are best pruned with secateurs in April and in August, and no more. *Lonicera nitida*, box and privet can be pruned by mechanical hedge-clippers or hand-shears, and from spring to late summer such trimming will be needed every few weeks. It is not wise to cut hedges back hard too late in the year, as this leaves them very bare in winter; but in the spring it does no harm to most hedge-plants if they are cut well back, leaving them only a foot or so wide. (This does not apply to conifers, which should not usually be cut back too far at the sides.) A slightly wedge-shape to the hedge—*i.e.*, a little extra width at the base—is desirable, as rain and light fall on the lower leaves, and the growth remains more uniform.

A word must be said here about hedge-planting. Young plants establish themselves best, and make a more uniform hedge than older plants. It is also a fact that after several years the young plants will outgrow the older ones, as they will have a better root-system.

Another point about planting is that slight protection in the early stages will make a hedge establish itself, and more than justify the extra labour of putting wattle hurdles or other protection in position. This is especially necessary near the seaside or in windswept positions.

THE USE OF SHRUBS AND TREES IN DESIGN

Whole books can be written about the use of trees and shrubs in the garden. Here we have room for only a few brief comments.

Both trees and shrubs are useful in all sorts of gardens as backgrounds to the pictures. One has but to glance at new gardens, where the picture appears to have two dimensions only, to realise what a difference height can make to the scene. Shrubs and trees are also useful as specimen plants on a small lawn or in large grounds. Small standard or half-standard trees of flowering type, such as the Japanese cherries, are useful in small gardens, or bush roses or lilacs, standard roses and climbing shrubs grown on pillars can be used for the same purpose in tiny town plots.

Shrubs and trees are also of use to those who do not wish to spend much time in a garden, but desire something pleasant and green to look at, with a minimum of effort. Grass that can be cut mechanically, and shrubs that can be left for long periods unattended, are ideal for such gardens.

Shrubs and trees of specially hardy type make fine windbreaks, when a garden must be made in a very exposed position. Such plantings should be the first steps taken in making seaside gardens or gardens on hilltops where winds are likely to be troublesome.

Shrubs and trees can be colourful and attractive at

all seasons. In spring there are the flowers, in summer leaves of various colours—especially where variegated

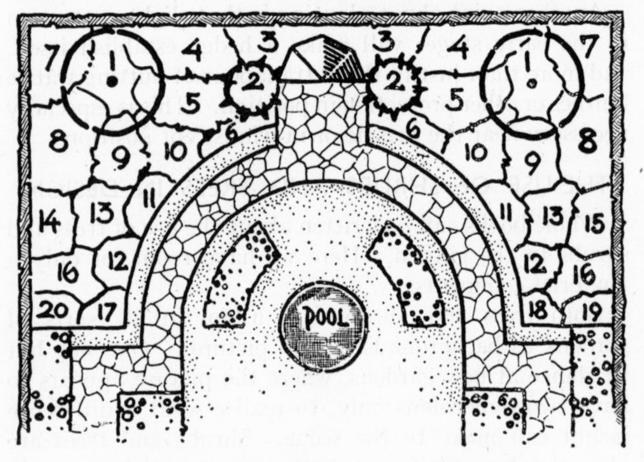

FIG. 51.—DESIGN FOR A SHRUB BORDER.

Key.		*No.*
1.	*Prunus triloba* (ST)	2
2.	*Cupressus Allumii glanca*	2
3.	*Laburnum Vossii*	4
4.	*Syringa vulgaris—in var.*	4
5.	*Fuchsia corallina*	8
6.	*Cotoneaster horizontalis*	6
7.	*Philadelphus virgina*	2
8.	*Forsythia int. spect.*	4
9.	*Rhododendron hybrida*	2
10.	*Hydrangea hortensis*	4
11.	*Spiraea Bumalda*	4
12.	*Azalea mollis*	1
13.	*Ribes sanguineum*	2
14.	*Viburnum op. sterile*	1
15.	*Buddleia var.*	1
16.	*Viburnum Carlesii*	1
17.	*Olearia Hastii*	4
18.	*Senecio Greyii*	4
19.	*Hamamelis*	1
20.	*Hamamelis*	1

maples and similar plants are used. In autumn the tints of leaf and berry make shrubs and trees the " high spot" in garden beauty. In winter there are bright evergreens, and the clever planter can display against their comforting background such beauties as the white-stemmed brambles, yellow- and red-stemmed dogwoods, light-green-stemmed Leycesteria, and the golden flowers of winter jasmine and *Hamamelis mollis*.

It must not be forgotten, too, that what the Americans call foundation planting—the planting that links house and garden—is done mainly with shrubs—wall-climbers, formal shrubs grown in boxes to stand against walls and near porches, porch climbers, and so on.

Finally, a word concerning the choice of shrubs and trees. Planters have to consider the soil, the aspect, the ultimate height, spread and general appearance of the fully grown shrub or tree, and the question of successional beauty. All the year round shrubs and trees flourish, but their greatest beauty is seasonal, and the aim of the planter should be to have some shrub-beauty present at all seasons. Lists given in this book will help in plant selection, but nurserymen's catalogues are also useful. For large planting schemes plans should be drawn up on paper, and consultation with an expert is generally advisable.

LAWNS

Mention has been made of the beauty of shrubs, trees and grass, and the possibility for busy garden-owners of making labour-saving gardens of these plants only. This is, therefore, the proper place to talk of lawns, which form so characteristic a part in British garden-making.

Whole books have been written about lawns, but although there is much to learn, the general principles of lawn-making and lawn-care can be briefly outlined. I suggest that the first thing a gardening student needs to note in this connexion is that *a lawn is a collection of plants.* This rather obvious statement is apt to be forgotten even by experienced gardeners, who roll lawns in wet weather until the plants are "cemented" in and unable to breathe, or cut them so close to the ground that they are left almost no foliage, forgetting that in this way they are unable to feed themselves properly, and must be assisted by regular artificial feeding. Another common fault is rough raking, which tears grass-plants up by the roots, in addition to removing moss and leaves. A good gardener treats grass with respect, just as he treats his border plants.

In making lawns, the first care should be drainage and the preparation of a level surface. Land drains are rarely necessary, but should be laid down, if needed, during the levelling of the site. Trenches cut herring-bone fashion and filled at the bottom with about 4 inches of rough, porous material, which is covered with about 8 inches of good soil, are sufficient to drain most lawn sites satisfactorily. The trenches will drain the soil for a distance of perhaps 15 feet on each side.

Levelling for lawn-making should be thought out before hand. The ideal is to leave the old top soil layer of dark, fertile soil still at the surface, because this layer will feed the grass and make the lawn grow well. If, therefore, a lawn has to be made dead level on a site that slopes steeply, one half of the lawn should be tackled at a time. First the soil from one half should be stripped off to a depth of about 10 inches (dividing the plot in line with the slope) and piled on to the other half in a long ridge. Then the subsoil from the higher end will be dug out and wheeled to the lower end until the surface is roughly level. The top soil can then be redistributed over the level patch. The second half can then be treated in the same way. This method lessens the labour of soil removal.

Levelling should be done with the help of pegs painted white for a distance of, say, a foot from the top. These can be driven in at intervals, and the tops levelled with the help of a spirit-level and a straight-edge. An easy way is to use a stout piece of two by two, to which the spirit-level is tied. Lay this from peg to peg as the levelling proceeds.

Remember that the part of a lawn made on a sloping hillside that will be generally wettest is the end from which the soil has been excavated during levelling, while the end of the lawn that was built up will be relatively drier. A little extra stable manure or leaf-mould used at the dry end and a few extra trench drains cut in the subsoil at the damp end will help to make the lawn develop uniformly.

Whether a lawn is made from turf or by seed-sowing, the initial preparation should be the same, for both require good drainage and a level surface. There is not so much need to trouble about soil fertility if turf is laid down, as the turf is established, and with top feeding occasionally, it will grow well. In the case of sown lawns, it is essential that the most fertile soil should be in the top layer, and a good deal of preparation before sowing will be found to pay. For the best results a lawn to be sown should be either prepared in autumn and sown in spring, or prepared during the spring and sown in September.

Turf Laying. A lawn of high quality can be made from high-quality turf, but this is expensive. A very inferior lawn is made from turf that is not of the highest quality, and in the small garden it would be far better to use seed than to buy cheap turves. Cumberland turf, weed free, and composed of the finest lawn grasses, is ideal. Preparation for this should consist (on levelled sites) of digging to a depth of 9 inches. At the same time some well-rotted manure, if available, can be worked into the soil.

Level and roll the ground well; then, just before the turf is laid, rake the top very lightly. Turves cut 1 foot square and 2 inches thick are the easiest to handle, as they do not readily break, but larger turves are common.

FIG. 52.—Sea-washed turf makes the ideal lawn in a short time. It is cut in one foot squares, and laid in sand. More sea sand is brushed into the cracks, but rolling is delayed until the turves are knit together.

FIG. 53.—To repair a broken lawn edge, cut out a square of turf, turn it right round so that the broken edge is inside; then roll well.

In any case, for the best results the turves should be put down diagonally across the lawn, and bonded as are brick walls. Rolling will then be less likely to lift the turf.

For very even surfaces the ground is levelled accurately first, and as each turf is laid it is prepared by being placed in a wooden frame $1\frac{1}{2}$ inches deep and exactly the size of the turves, the soil on the underside of the turf being levelled off while it lies upside down in the frame. It is then reversed into position, and there should be almost no need for further adjustments in level after the whole lawn is complete. A little finely sifted soil should be handy to the worker, and this can be used to seal up cracks between the turves. The turves are watered after laying, and then rolled, and the level surface of the lawn tested with a spirit-level and straight-edge.

The best time to lay turf is in the autumn, though spring turfing can be quite satisfactory if the water supply is kept up through the summer. If laid in spring, the grass is likely to grow up rapidly, and it may be necessary to cut it with a scythe once or twice. If laid in autumn, the probability is that the mower will be able to be used in spring, without previous scything.

Seed-sowing. Digging to a depth of 9 inches and great care over the texture of the top few inches of soil are essential to success with seed-sowing. If old decayed manure cannot be used in digging, use some artificial fertiliser a week before sowing, raking this in when the surface is finally prepared for the seeds. Lawns will not thrive if the seed is sown on sour, acid soil, and on heavy, clay soils some lime should be used when preparing the ground. On light soils grass is said to grow better if lime is absent (but the soil should never be really acid), and if sulphate of ammonia is used exclusively as a fertiliser. This treatment results in the encouragement of finer grasses, and ultimately in a very good lawn.

Seed is sown at the rate of 1 oz. per square yard—a little more if a lawn is wanted very quickly, and a little less if time is unimportant, and in congenial rural districts. Seed is selected by seedsmen for various purposes and various soils, and if a large area is to be sown, it pays to obtain advice from the seedsman on this point.

To sow evenly, divide the lawn into strips, a yard wide, stretching the garden-line along the lawn for this purpose. Then, taking twice the number of ounces of seed that there are yards in the measured strip, sow this as evenly as possible along the strip. Rake lightly, and dust a little extra soil over before attending to the

FIG. 54.—Divide lawn seed into two, then sow first up and down the plot and then from side to side. This makes far more even distribution.

next yard-wide strip. In this way the site will all be sown without unnecessary treading. If the ground has been previously well rolled and prepared with a fine tilth on the top, it should be possible, on a dry sowing day, to walk over the unsown part of the lawn (in flat-bottomed shoes) without harm, but if the ground is too soft for this, a length of board can be used to stand on while sowing.

A light wooden roller over the sown surface will complete the operation; if no light roller is available, beat the surface with the flat blade of the spade, for this presses soil in close contact with the seeds, and so ensures even germination.

When the grass is about 1½ inches high, roll it again with the light roller, and a few days later make the first cut with the mower, setting the blades so that they just skim off the tips of the grass. Make quite sure that the moisture in the soil is not too great when you use the mower: seedlings pull easily from damp soil, and it may be better to wait and make the first cut with a scythe.

Care of a Lawn after it is established can be summed up in few words: roll frequently, whenever the soil is not too wet or too dry; use the mower as often as possible, a daily walk with it is good; watch for weeds and destroy them before they take hold of the site, and keep up the food supply.

With regard to weeds, a selective weedkiller is the modern answer. This cannot be used without some danger on newly sown turf, and a period of twelve weeks should elapse after either sowing or turfing before the weedkiller is applied. Moss on lawns is generally a sign of faulty drainage: if this is not the case, a dressing of soot and wood-ash in December, or the use of sulphate of iron and sand mixed, and applied so that only ¼ oz. of the sulphate of iron goes on to each square yard, will effect a cure.

A good home-made lawn-sand, to apply in autumn or spring over a lawn that is troubled with daisies and similar weeds, can be made with one part iron sulphate, three parts sulphate of ammonia, and thirty parts sand or sifted ash.

Clover on lawns is caused by a deficiency of nitrates in the soil. Dressings of sulphate of ammonia every few weeks in spring and early summer will put matters right.

Large, tap-rooted weeds, such as dandelions, are best pulled out, or cut out, a spot of strong carbolic (1 oz. to a gallon of water) being dropped on to the remaining root-stump. Special tools for this purpose are sold, and where large old lawns have to be reconditioned these tools are worth while. In small patches an old knife will serve the purpose.

Lawn Repairs. Old lawns develop hollows and humps, and the edges get broken down and untidy. Repairs of this kind should be made by lifting pieces of turf where the fault occurs. A special tool for this purpose is also available, but a spade can be made to serve. Lift the turf, take out or add soil as required, and replace the turf, to repair hollows and humps. Lift the turf, and turn it round so that a straight edge goes to the outside, if broken edges are to be repaired.

Bare patches on lawns (which may be caused by wear, or by leatherjackets) can be resown, after light forking, just as seed is sown for a new lawn. Where pests have been at work, some form of insecticide must be used to prevent further damage. (See also Chapter XIII, on Pests and Diseases.)

DIARY OF THE FLOWER PATCH

January

Prepare a detailed plan for each flower border and bed. Order flower seeds. Dress with bonemeal any vacant beds, fork this in, and then dust the surface with lime (2–4 oz. bonemeal to the square yard and 1–2 oz. garden lime to the square yard.)

Sow under glass sweet peas, dahlias, Japanese chrysanthemums, and other flowers that like a long period of growth before flowering. If no heat is available, delay sowings until February or March.

Start stored dahlias in heat, to produce cuttings next month.

February

Top dress perennial borders with old rotted manure. Plant roses and other deciduous shrubs.

Sow in frames (or greenhouse) antirrhinums, China asters, lobelia, zinnia, alyssum, petunias and other half-hardy annuals.

Start bedding geraniums, fuchsias, etc., into new growth by giving more water and more light and heat.

Prune late flowering shrubs.

March

Renovate old mixed and herbaceous borders. Clean up and fork beds where annuals are to be sown. Fork lightly between bulbs.

Sow hardy annuals in the open garden—clarkia, candytuft, collinsia, eschscholtzia, gaillardia, love-in-a-mist, nemophila, mignonette, poppies, night-scented stock, Virginian stocks, etc. Sow sweet peas, if not sown already under glass.

Plant out hardy plants such as rooted carnation layers, chrysanthemums, pansies, violas, etc.

Sow under glass (in frames, or cloches) antirrhinums and similar near-hardy flowers.

Take cuttings under glass, and pot on rooted cuttings of dahlias, geraniums, etc., as needed.

Prune roses.

April

Use slug-killer where seedlings are sown in the open. Keep the hoe going wherever possible.

Sow annuals—half-hardy annuals may be sown outdoors towards the end of the month, including nasturtiums, cosmea, star of the veldt, venidium, ursinia, brachycome and phlox drummondii.

Plant out sweet peas, antirrhinums, carnations, and other seedlings raised under glass, if the weather is suitable. Do not plant out tender seedlings, such as zinnias, until later.

Take cuttings of dahlias and other plants under glass, to raise enough plants for bedding out in late May.

May

Finish all planting for the season by the end of the month. Tender subjects, such as dahlias, geraniums, zinnias, heliotropes, and other summer bedding plants should not be set out until all danger of frost is past.

Sow biennials and perennials as convenient, including columbines, hardy primulas, brompton stocks, forget-me-nots, canterbury bells, foxgloves, honesty, wall-flowers, scabious, lupins, delphiniums, catananche, and perennial flax.

Set stakes in position in the mixed and herbaceous borders.

Thin out annuals as needed. Some, such as love-in-a-mist, may be transplanted: others, such as Shirley poppies, can only be thinned.

A frame or handlight is useful for sowing hardy primulas and other seeds that need some care.

June

Hoe as required, and if watering is necessary, do this in the evenings.

Use insecticides to keep down greenfly and other pests.

If bedding out is incomplete, it should be finished without delay.

Early-flowering perennials should be cut down as the flowers fade unless seed is desired. Anchusa, doronicums, lupins, etc., if cut back now may flower a second time.

Seeds of biennials can still be sown. Seeds of perennials should be sown in a nursery plot. Home-saved seed germinates well, but may not produce worth-while plants: if used, sow as soon as gathered.

Cuttings of such subjects as double-flowered wall-flowers, special colours in sweet williams, double arabis, etc., should be taken now.

Stop chrysanthemums and dahlias as needed; sweet peas should be restricted to one or two main stems, all side growths being nipped out.

Sow rock plants—carnations, pinks, aubretia, candy-tuft, saxifrages, etc.—in the frame or greenhouse.

July

Hoe, weed, and water as needed.

Top-dress shrubs, roses and other plants if possible, using leafy soil or old rotted compost.

Stop chrysanthemums, layer carnations, take cuttings of pinks and other early flowering perennials, including most of the rock plants of smother growth, such as aubretia.

Sow more perennials, including hollyhocks and violas.

Plant out seedlings of biennials and perennials to allow sufficient room for growth.

Take more cuttings, including rose-cuttings, under glass.

August

Clear away dead tops, leaves, etc., from the borders and attend to staking where needed.

Layer and take cuttings of any suitable plants: roots form rapidly at this season, while the soil is warm.

Plant colchicums, and a few of the earlier flowering narcissi, if available.

Replant old bulbs in grass, or in the wild garden, if they are not of sufficient size to use for spring bedding.

Sow hardy annuals in pots, for winter flowering, and prepare a bed outdoors, in a sheltered position, for a few early annuals next spring. Sow outdoors at the end of the month.

September

Collect ripe seeds, tidy up the borders and carry all rubbish to the compost heap.

Train in all climbers, and stake late-flowering border flowers: autumn winds may cause trouble.

Sow very hardy annuals in the open garden, to bloom in early summer. Candytuft, clarkia, larkspur, love-in-a-mist, annual chrysanthemums and Californian poppies are good subjects for autumn sowing. Antirrhinums sown now in the nursery bed may stand the winter, and if so they will make excellent bedding plants.

Take cuttings of bedding plants, in boxes, to winter under glass.

Plant spring-flowering bulbs, except tulips, which should be planted later.

Sow pansies and violas in a nurserybed.

Plant evergreens.

Sow new lawns in showery weather.

October

Renovate herbaceous borders as soon as the flowers fade.

Prepare plans for any large alterations that are to be made in the flower garden, in the number and shape of beds, and in the size and extent of the rock garden.

If possible, repair all paths before the frosty weather.

Plant herbaceous perennials of all kinds and also deciduous shrubs, whether specimens or for hedging.

Lift and divide old perennials, and take cuttings of woody subjects such as lavender, sage, etc.

Sow sweet peas to stand the winter: choose a sheltered position.

Plant out biennial seedlings in their permanent positions. Also plant out perennial seedlings that have grown large enough for the borders.

November

Sweep up leaves and take them to the compost heap. Tidy all borders and paths.

Put in position any protective material, such as evergreen twigs among the tea roses, or dry bracken among the peonies.

Tie together the foliage of red hot pokers, and pampas grass, to protect the crowns. Peonies can be increased by division of the roots now, but some protection should be given after separating the crowns, specially if early frosts are troublesome.

Finish planting all spring bulbs, and set out plants intended for spring bedding while the soil is frost free.

December

Keep an eye on the beds and borders if the weather is exceptionally bad: do not allow snow to damage evergreens. Otherwise concentrate on indoor jobs.

Sterilize materials and prepare potting and seed sowing composts.

Prepare plans for the next summer. Paint over old wooden labels. Make out seed lists. Wash pots and other utensils in the greenhouse. Take stock of tools, and see that everything is ready for the New Year.

CHAPTER X

FRUIT

The cultivation of fruit on a large scale is naturally a commercial proposition, and comes outside the scope of this book. Every student of gardening, however, wants to know sufficient on this subject to cultivate fruits for home consumption—that is, he wants to know how to obtain, plant and care for ordinary garden fruits, and to understand the principles that underlie these routine tasks.

Let us first consider the choice of fruits. The size of the plot to be filled affects this: in a small garden, where only a limited number of fruits can be planted, the grower will be wise to choose fruits that are either expensive to buy or difficult to obtain in fresh condition. Raspberries and other soft fruits travel badly, and those offered in shops can never be of the prime quality that should be present in home-grown fruits.

Another point affecting choice is the size and constitution of the family. Apples which fruit regularly and well, and which, if properly selected, can be grown to provide a succession of fruit practically all the year round, are a good choice where a family of youngsters are to be provided for.

Then there is the question of soil and aspect and protection. Soil can, in a small garden, be improved and altered so much that this need not be an obstacle to the cultivation of any desired fruit. In gardens where the plants will be heavily shaded for a great part of the day, gooseberries might thrive and fruit very well, but peaches and nectarines certainly would not: sunshine is essential to the peach, and a wall facing south is really the only satisfactory position for this fruit in the open. In a very cold, windswept fruit-garden a line of damsons along the coldest side makes a good protection, for these fruits are very hardy, and rarely fail to give a good account of themselves, while their presence breaks the winds, and so protects other fruits.

FIG. 55.—Blossom-time in the fruit orchard.

Choice of fruits means not only choice of kinds (and varieties), but also a choice of types. Orchard fruits are grown as bushes, standards, pyramids, and as cordons, espaliers and fan-trained, the last three types being trained to walls or to wires strained between stout posts. Naturally the choice of such types will vary according to the positions available. Small gardens rarely accommodate the very large standards that are found in commercial plantations (of cherries, for instance), not only because of their size, but also because of difficulties of picking the fruit. Smaller standard trees are, however, sometimes preferable to bushes, as some planting can be done under the standard tree. Small standards are definitely created by the choice of stocks of dwarfing nature, and fruit-planters should, because of this, always take the nurseryman into their confidence when selecting trees, for he alone knows what can be expected of the plants he offers. Grafting and budding—methods of creating fruit of the desired type—have already been described in Chapter VIII. Soil improvement and hints on planting have also been treated in previous chapters: there is no essential difference between the planting of a fruit tree and the planting of an ornamental shrub or tree. Here, therefore, we shall pass straight to the treatment of individual fruits. Students of gardening who wish to apply in a practical way the information given concerning each fruit, are recommended to practise laying out (on paper) fruit-gardens in various sized plots, for various-sized families. A glance at the plan given (see p. 30) will show how fruits can be arranged to allow the needed space and sunshine for the different kinds. It is also worth while to practise planning for development. That is, fruit trees can be so planted that quick-maturing kinds occupy temporarily the space that will later be required by larger trees: gooseberries could be grown between bush-apples, for instance, until the apples become large enough to need all the space allotted. Care must be taken that in each planting plan the full needs of the various fruits can be met.

NOTE REGARDING FIG. 58 (see p. 147).

This shows an espalier-trained tree (neglect has caused the bad development of the fourth and fifth horizontal branches). It will now be necessary to prune the upper part severely so as to restore the tree to its proper form. The side stems should not extend beyond the branches that are immediately below.

FIG. 56.—Fan-trained fig on wall.

FIG. 57.—Half-standard tree. FIG. 58 *.—Espalier-trained tree.

* See footnote on p. 146.

FIG. 59.—Note the fatter appearance of flower buds (centre) while the formant leaf buds are slim and pointed (top growth).

FIG. 60.—Pear tree showing a stem that grows in towards the centre. This must be pruned away to allow the development of a "goblet" shaped skeleton.

APPLES

Good deep loam is best for apples, but any soil, improved by methods suggested in Chapter V, will grow apples. In reasonably good soil, plant without using manure, plant firmly and stake the tree, whether it be bush, standard or cordon, at planting time.

Apples grown on dwarfing stocks will make early fruiting, useful trees for small gardens: trees can be set 10 feet apart, if bushes or pyramids, and up to 25 feet apart if to be grown as standards (the larger space for trees on crab stock where large trees are wanted). Plant espaliers on walls 15 feet apart. Plant cordons 30 inches apart (single cordons), and train them obliquely, as this induces greater fruitfulness.

At planting time no pruning should be needed, unless it is desirable to cut back a damaged branch. The following summer look over the new wood that has grown since planting, and shorten the side shoots (that is, those that grow out of the old wood along the side of the stem), leaving only a few inches of new growth. Make the cut just above a leaf-bud—which is a dormant bud, generally very small and pointed. Fruit-buds are wide, round and flattish in comparison. Do not, in summer, shorten the main branches at all, but in winter go over the trees again, shorten the side-stems to half the length left at the summer pruning, and at the same time shorten the main branches. In doing this remove more or less of their new growth, according to its appearance. You want every branch of your apple tree to become like a single cordon—that is, with fruit-spurs placed close together all along the branch. If possible, too, you want a tree to develop symmetrically, and to be of such a shape that the lower branches as well as the upper ones receive their share of sun. Over-long branches are therefore pruned well back, care being taken to leave at the end of the pruned stem a bud pointing in the direction in which a new stem is to grow.

Trees treated in this way will eventually become shapely, with branches each resembling the stem of a single cordon. There are, however, some exceptions to be made in pruning. Certain apples, known as tip-bearers, do not readily make fruiting spurs close to the old wood, which is the main object of the pruning method described. They tend, especially while young, to carry their flowers and fruits at the tip of side-growths. In pruning these most of the young side-growths are left full length, as otherwise the flower-bud is removed. Long side-growths must be shortened, or the trees become overcrowded, and fail to flower through lack of sunshine. (Grenadier, Bismarck, Beauty of Bath, Worcester Pearmain and Bramley's Seedling are tip-bearers.)

Just one other point *re* pruning: fruits, specially apples, often suffer more from over-pruning than from under-pruning. The natural habit of a tree is to flower and fruit freely, and, left alone, most trees will perform this task. The aim of the pruner is just to speed up flower production, and to improve the quality of the fruit. Over-pruning often leads to the formation of more leaf and stem, and consequent delay in fruiting. If in doubt, therefore, the wise gardener will limit pruning to the removal of broken, diseased or obviously unwanted branches, preventing crowding, and crossing of stems, and letting light in to all parts of the tree.

The selection of apple varieties in a small garden is a matter of real concern. Nearly all fruits thrive best when cross-pollination can take place—that is, when other fruits are grown near, and pollen can be freely carried by insects from one variety to another. Apples are particularly influenced by cross-pollination, and even so-called self-fertile varieties often set much more fruit when cross-pollination takes place. Nurserymen are now adopting the practice of grafting more than one variety on the same stock. This produces a tree that can cross pollinate itself and should therefore produce plenty of fruit even when grown in complete isolation. This " Family Tree " should be sought whenever a single tree only can be grown in a small garden.

PEARS

Just as apples are grafted on to crab stock for large commercial orchards and on to dwarfing Paradise stock for small gardens, so pears are grafted on to wild pear if large specimens are wanted, and on to quince if a smaller tree, suitable for a little garden, is needed. Pears are sometimes double-grafted—that is, grafted a second time—so that actually three trees go to the making of one, and the influence of all three is felt.

Choice, planting and cultivation of pears are practically the same as for apples, and need not be repeated. A good deal of discretion must be used in pruning, for pears grow naturally to very different shapes, some spreading and loose, while others form a natural compact pyramid. In this they are like cherries, some of which need practically no pruning to form a symmetrical tree, while others need the use of the knife in their young stages. A few pears, like Jargonelle, are tip bearers, and are pruned accordingly.

Almost all pears need cross-pollination to become fully fruitful, and at least two trees should be grown. Laxton's Superb, and Williams, for instance, both flowering at about the same time, would make a good pair.

PLUMS AND DAMSONS

Half-standards, standards, bushes and fan-trained wall-trees are the types of plums grown. Half-standards are very useful for small front gardens, where a decorative tree is required. Fan-trees should be allowed 15 feet of wall space, bushes and half-standards need 10 feet, and standards 25.

Pruning of plums in the early stages, to make a shapely tree, is desirable, but in later life it is generally best to do as little pruning as possible. In the case of wall trees and trees that tend to make too much slender growth so that the tree is crowded, some summer pruning on similar lines to that practised on apples and pears is helpful. It is wiser to prune with finger and thumb—that is, to prune, if at all, while the growth is still young. Wounds made in older wood are apt to allow disease germs to enter. All pruning-cuts should be sealed over with white lead paint to avoid trouble. Winter pruning should be done in *late* winter.

Victoria plums are probably the best for small gardens; they are self-fertile, and can be planted alone with every prospect of success. There are a great many other plums that are equally satisfactory as regards pollination, and selection from growers' catalogues is simple.

CHERRIES

Cherries are perhaps the most temperamental of all the common fruits when it comes to soil conditions, and good cherry trees are difficult to cultivate outside the noted cherry districts. The trees are large, and their roots spread so far that it would not be easy to substitute soil for their needs. Standard trees are set 40 feet apart, bush or fan-shaped trees 12 feet apart.

Sweet cherries and sour cooking cherries are treated

in different ways. Sweet cherries are not self-fertile, and must always be planted in pairs of varieties. Pruning of these cherries should be restricted to the removal of unwanted, diseased or broken wood, when once the desired head has been formed to the tree.

Morello cherries are the best for wall culture. These can be pruned after the manner of other cordon fruits, and will respond by gradually forming spurs. Where the trees are grown as standards or bushes, pruning will consist only of occasional removal of old wood to encourage the development of new wood. All pruning-cuts should be painted over (as plums) to prevent disease. As with plums, leave pruning until late in winter, except that dead wood can be cut out at the time of leaf-fall, or, if preferred, immediately the fruit has been gathered.

APRICOTS

Ordinary garden soil, but with exceptionally good drainage, suits the apricot. On the whole, a dry situation is preferable. Fan-shaped trees, four years old, are the best for small gardens, and these should occupy a position on a south or south-west wall. Allow 15 feet of wall space.

Pruning of apricots is important. Remove entirely shoots that grow outwards at right angles from the wall, in summer. Also take out weak shoots, and prevent overcrowding. Tie in healthy growths to the support. If cordon plants are grown (30 inches apart) nip back the side growths in July, leaving six buds, and cut back in winter.

In winter thin out weak wood, and if the tree is growing too far in one direction, restore its shape by cutting back the leaders to a point where a new stem is growing, lower down.

PEACHES AND NECTARINES

Bush-trees are suitable only for the very mildest districts, but peaches and nectarines can be grown successfully in warm gardens on south or south-west walls. Plant fan-shaped trees in autumn, allowing 15 feet of wall space (four-year-old trees).

Peaches flower on the previous season's strong growths (and on spurs, if present). No pruning is needed on bush-trees, but wall-fruits need a good deal of care. In training a fan on a wall, encourage the lower branches first, and remove the strong centre branch, if it is present: otherwise the tree will develop upwards and lose its fan shape. A trellis or wires fixed a distance of a few inches from the wall is the best support for peaches. Remove the older side-growths in winter, after the whole tree has been treated with insecticide. Tie in the young side-growths: in a perfectly grown tree the branches of the fan would each resemble a herringbone, with side-stems (to carry the fruit) growing out on each side, at regular intervals. This is the aim of the pruner, and he should get as near it as possible. Then, in early summer, a number of laterals will grow out from these side-stems: these are not all wanted, and so all except one shoot at the base of the fruiting stem are generally rubbed off as they begin to develop. This is to encourage the development of just one fresh shoot to take the place of the old fruiting stem which will be cut away in winter.

GRAPES

Outdoor grape-vines are often considered as ornamental vines only, and for this reason pruning is neglected. This is a pity, for the picture of bunches of grapes hanging among the decorative foliage is charming in itself, while the fruits, in sunny seasons, have a flavour that most people appreciate.

Plant grapes against a south wall, and prepare the site by deep digging, and mixing into the soil plenty of coarse bonemeal and mortar rubble, and any available bonfire ash.

To form a young plant, allow only the strongest stem to develop, and tie this to its support. In the following January cut this back about half-way. As it grows, train the top shoot upwards in place of the part removed; meanwhile "stop" the side-shoots on the lower part of the plant when four or five leaves have formed.

If a good deal of wall is to be covered, allow three of the top buds to develop instead of one, and spread these out as desired. They can be allowed to branch still more, according to the wishes of the cultivator. In every season, however, the stems that are not wanted to build up a larger framework are all stopped when four or five leaves have developed, if they do not show flower-trusses; but if flowers form, the tip of the shoot is pinched off at a point just beyond the second leaf above the flower-truss. At the same time, if desired, tendrils can be cut away: vines are either trained to wires, or secured by the use of wall-nails.

FIGS

The best time to plant a fig is in November, and the best site is against a warm wall, in well-drained soil. Trees of bush or standard type in sheltered gardens, where good soil overlies chalky subsoil, often thrive well.

A four-year-old, fan-trained tree, or a well-formed standard or bush will need little pruning, except the removal of weak shoots, and the summer trimming of side shoots, to admit light and air.

Regular hoeing, to keep a surface of dusty soil round

the tree, is almost the only special cultivation needed: winter spraying is not required.

NUTS

Nuts cultivated in British gardens include cobnuts, filberts and walnuts. Walnuts are usually planted as standards or half-standards, though bushes have been planted recently. They are deep-rooters, and need good, rich loam and plenty of moisture during the first few summers after planting. The walnut is slightly tender, and will not bear nuts if exposed to heavy frosts. It takes a considerable time for a tree to reach fruiting stage, and it is generally supposed that walnuts are only planted for the coming generations.

Cobnuts and filberts, on the other hand, begin to bear fruit very quickly after planting. They succeed in almost any soil and situation, but prefer good soil and sunshine.

Pruning of cobnuts is done in March, long growths being shortened much as are the side-growths on apples, care being taken not to remove those stems that are carrying the female flowers. In addition, suckers should be cut away, and old, woody, short stems that have no flowers present should also be removed.

The difference between cobnuts and filberts is only in the length of the husk: if it comes only part way up the nut, it is a cobnut, whereas in the filbert the nut is completely covered.

It is worth noting that some nuts are not self-fertile, and unless there are wild nuts growing near, several different nuts should be planted together.

CURRANTS

All currants—black, white and red—are best grown for general purposes as bushes, and for this purpose they are planted 5 feet apart. Plant as for ordinary flowering shrubs, remembering that black currants prefer a rather moist loam. In fact, black currants are known to thrive in riverside gardens where annual flooding takes place.

Red and white currants are pruned in winter in similar manner to apples, and a certain amount of summer pruning, on the same lines—that is, shortening the side-growths to prevent overcrowding and encourage " spurs " —is also desirable. Black currants, on the other hand, fruit on young wood of one year old, and pruning in their case is done immediately after the fruit is gathered. At this time the old wood is cut hard back, to allow fresh new shoots to grow and carry the next season's crop. Good feeding must accompany the hard pruning, or the crops will be small.

Some growers like to cut back their black currants to within a few inches of the ground every other season, treating alternate plants in this way, so that the plant gets an opportunity to make good growth before it is drastically pruned again.

With all currants, and also gooseberries, it is best to cut back the plant hard in the first planting year, thus sacrificing one season's fruit for the sake of the years to follow.

GOOSEBERRIES

These also are planted 5 feet apart (as with currants) and pruned rather hard in the first season. Gooseberries will fruit on young or old wood, and pruning, which is generally done at the end of winter, should be designed to leave the most promising stems of young or old wood. A little summer pruning of side-growths is also helpful where bushes tend to become crowded.

Propagation of currants and gooseberries is very

simply carried out by means of cuttings. In the case of black currants, pieces of stem are inserted without any special preparation, the cut being made just below a leaf joint. In the case of red and white currants and gooseberries, it is desirable to produce a plant with a short main stem free from side-growths, and supporting a " head "—*i.e.*, a plant like a standard, but on a short leg. In preparing the cuttings of these fruits all dormant buds on the lower part of the cutting are therefore removed before the cutting is inserted.

Cuttings inserted in autumn in the open garden can often be moved to fruiting quarters the following autumn, but it is sometimes advisable to leave them for two years undisturbed.

RASPBERRIES

Raspberries grow in the fashion of rambler roses: they produce a number of strong new canes from the ground-level each season, and these canes, after once fruiting, are cut away, leaving only new ones to carry on another season. In the case of summer-fruiting raspberries all the new canes are cut away to the ground-level immediately the fruit is gathered. Autumn-fruiting varieties are pruned hard back in winter: they produce fruit in autumn on canes that grow during the early part of the year. " Lloyd George " raspberries, if cut only half-way back after the summer fruiting, will bear some autumn fruit on the same canes, but it is doubtful if this method is to be encouraged, as the production of autumn fruit must weaken the canes that are growing for the next season.

Raspberries increase freely by suckers: at pruning time the plants should be overlooked, and only enough canes to carry the next season's crop should be retained. The unwanted suckers can be moved, if desired, to a new plantation. There they are planted in rows, 18 inches apart, or in groups of three, with 4 feet between the groups.

Do not use tar-oil sprays on raspberries in winter.

LOGANBERRIES AND SIMILAR BERRIES

Loganberries, blackberries, lowberries and so on are grown very like raspberries, but more space is allowed them. As a rule they are planted 10 feet apart against walls or fences, or where wires strained between posts can be used for their support.

Pruning is as for rambler roses: all old canes are cut away in autumn, and new ones tied in their place.

STRAWBERRIES

Cleared woodland is said to be the ideal home for strawberries, but any good garden soil in an open, sunny position will do. Strawberries are planted in September, or, occasionally, in March. Set the plants carefully, 18 inches apart, allowing from 2 to 3 feet between the rows. Use a trowel for planting, and make the roots quite firm in the soil.

Most strawberries are self-fertile, but in case of unusual varieties being grown, a row of " Royal Sovereign " here and there in the strawberry patch will make certain on this point.

A good practice is to renew one-third of a strawberry patch each year: as the plants fruit best in the second and third years, this ensures a regular crop. New plants can be bought from a reliable nurseryman, or, if raised at home, they should be rooted in a special propagating bed which is kept free from disease by constant watching and removal of doubtful plants. The method of increase is by layers, or runners. These, in any strawberry plot, appear in large numbers. To secure the best plants, pots are sunk to the rim in the soil near the maiden plant, and filled with good potting soil. The runner is then pegged down into the pot of soil, where roots form freely. The connecting stem between old and new plant is then severed, and the runner, in its pot, grown on until planting time. It is considered best to raise runners in this way in a separate bed, away from the fruiting plants, and to cut off, immediately they are seen, any runners that the fruiting plants produce, but in a small garden runners are more often taken from the plants that are bearing good fruit. If taken from fruiting plants, only one or at most two runners should be allowed to each plant: in a nursery bed a plant can be allowed to produce an indefinite number of runners (100 from a plant at times !).

Regular hoeing all the summer, autumn and winter, and until straw or mats are put in position, is required to keep the plants healthy. A little fertiliser dusted along the rows when the flowers are open, and hoed in, should precede the strawing. Straw laid round the plants keeps the fruit from getting soiled. After the fruit is gathered this straw can be burnt where it is: it will not do any damage to the plants.

QUINCES AND OTHER FRUITS

Quinces, medlars, mulberries and the decorative but edible crabs are fruits that need not be considered here except as ornamental trees and bushes. They are not sufficiently profitable to be regarded as commercial fruits, or even as orchard subjects; but there is something to be said in their favour, and the large garden should have its specimen of each. Pruning and cultivation can, however, be left to the common sense and practical experience of the gardener, for they will depend partly on what he wants from the tree—decoration or show fruits. Quinces are useful on damp soils, and best grown with a single stem from the ground-level. Medlars like a warm, drying soil. Mulberries are slightly tender, especially when young, and spring planting, with as little root damage as possible, is a wise precaution.

FRUIT-GROWERS' PROBLEMS

All problems and difficulties of the fruit-grower are summed up in the words " failure to bear fruit ". Let us, then, look at some of the reasons why fruit trees fail in their task. We can summarise them as follows:—

1. General weakness due to a weak root-system, or due to lack of food supplies.
2. Lack of blossom, due to ill-balanced food supplies.
3. Destruction of blossom or fruit, or general weakness caused by pests.
4. Disease, by infection through the agency of some pest, or through careless cultivation.

Let us take these in turn. General weakness due to a weak root-system is often the result of careless planting. If roots are severely damaged it will take a tree some time to establish itself. All torn roots should be cut cleanly away at planting time, and care should be taken that soft, friable loam is in contact with remaining roots. In this the tree can make fresh, fibrous roots if these have been damaged, but in sticky clay or hard, unfriendly soil root-hairs do not form freely, and the plant is unable to feed itself. Far less frequently is the soil so poor that the trees cannot establish themselves, and fertilisers are rarely needed until after the first year, if reasonably good soil exists at the outset. With older trees, however, an occasional dusting of general garden fertiliser round them will often bring a non-fruitful tree into bearing.

Lack of blossom, on a tree that grows well and looks healthy, is a sign that nitrogenous food is freely available but phosphates are in short supply. The remedy is to use some form of phosphatic fertiliser—basic slag on heavy soil in autumn, or superphosphate in spring on light soils. Bonemeal hoed in round the base of the tree is also useful. Lack of potash may also be a cause of trouble, particularly with apples. The use of potash salts, wood-ash and, on heavy soils, a dressing of lime are ways in which potash supplies can be made available to the tree.

Fruit-tree pests are far too numerous to be dealt with exhaustively here. A number of them are described in Chapter XIII. Here we will concern ourselves with routine operations that will keep down pests and diseases in the small orchard. Most pests are active in summer, and hibernate, or remain as dormant eggs, in winter. One of the best ways to control pests is the comparatively modern method of using a tar-distillate spray, and the best time to use this is between the middle of November and the middle of January. All fruits, except cobnuts, figs and strawberries, can be sprayed with winter wash (raspberries need not be sprayed with tar oil, and some prefer never to spray them), and the wash will destroy eggs of aphis (many types), apple sucker and several other pests.

In addition to spraying with tar oil, apples, pears and plums can be sprayed in winter with a Petroleum wash (Dinitro-cresol-petroleum oil), which is sold under various proprietary names and must be used strictly according to the makers' instructions. This spray kills the eggs of red spider, capsid bug and winter moth—all serious pests that have been difficult to control in the past.

In spite of care over winter washes, some pests will appear in summer, and the chief modern method of control for these is the use of derris in powder or liquid form. Derris is not poisonous to humans, and it can be freely used at any season. It is particularly effective against aphis, and against the beetles that cause trouble in the raspberry patch. D.D.T. sprays are also useful.

Diseases are also mainly controlled by spraying, either with lime sulphur or with Bordeaux mixture. In rare cases diseases are caused through shortage of some necessary food, but more often they are the result of infection. Great care over the control of pests, which are carriers of disease, is one of the most important ways of preventing trouble.

Lime sulphur and Bordeaux mixture are both sold in prepared form, and with them the makers give explicit instructions for their use. Lime sulphur will cure or control such diseases as apple-blossom wilt, scab, mildew, and will also control big bud on black currants. Serious diseases that cannot be cured are these:—

Apple Canker, showing as an open, nasty-looking wound. The canker must be cut out and the wound painted over to avoid further trouble.

Silver Leaf. A disease found mostly on plums. If the characteristic silvery appearance of foliage is noticed, the branch must be removed entirely to where no brown stain shows in the centre. Paint over at once the wounds made by the saw. Silver leaf is the subject of an order made by the Ministry of Agriculture, which insists that all dead wood must be removed and burnt each year before the middle of July.

For further remarks *re* pests and diseases, see Chapter XIII.

FRUITS MOST SUITABLE FOR VARIOUS SOILS

Light and Porous Soil

(a) Chalk (shallow topsoil)

Black currants.	Gooseberries.
Red currants.	Plums.
White currants.	Raspberries.
Damsons.	Strawberries.
Figs.	

(b) Chalk (deep topsoil).

As (a) above.	Mulberry.
Apples.	Quince.

(c) Sand.

As (*a*) above.
Cherries.
Nuts.

Light Soil but Retentive of Moisture

All fruits, including apricot, peach, nectarine, and wall grapes.

Heavy Soil, Well Drained

Apple.	Mulberry.
Blackberry.	Pears.
Black currant.	Plums.
Gooseberries.	Quince.
Medlar.	

Heavy Soil, with Poor Drainage

Apples (culinary).	Pears.
Black currants.	Plums.

Note that in every case some attempt must be made to improve the natural condition of the soil before planting.

Varieties of Popular Fruits for Small Gardens

Apples. Ellison's Orange (dessert), Crawley Beauty (culinary) or Rev. W. Wilks (culinary) where only one can be planted.

Small orchard selection: James Grieve, Ellison's Orange, Laxton's Superb for dessert, Lord Derby, Lane's Prince Albert, Rev. W. Wilks, Crawley Beauty for cooking.

Pears. Conference, Marie Louise, Dr. Jules Guyot, Williams Bon Chretien. (Any one will do alone.)

Plums. Victoria, alone, or Victoria, Czar, Giant Prune and Purple Pershore.

Cherries. Morello. If for large orchard, select from the Fertility (cross pollination) lists.

CROSS POLLINATION AND FRUIT FERTILITY

Most amateur gardeners today know a little about fruit fertility. They know that an isolated fruit tree will sometimes fail to bear any fruit, and that the planting, near to it, of a different variety, will make it immediately fruitful.

The subject is, however, a little more complicated than this simple statement would suggest. Take, for instance, the case of sweet cherries. If you planted Bedford Prolific and Elton Heart together, you might still have no fruit, since one flowers early and the other late, so that there might be no opportunity for cross-pollination. But again, you might plant Bedford Prolific with Early Rivers, and have flowers on both at the same time, and still not effect cross-pollination, since these two varieties are incompatible. Cherries naturally fall into groups, and as a rule varieties in the same group are useless as pollinators of each other. So, in large planting schemes, it is absolutely necessary to study the group classification.

In the case of apples, pears, and plums also, there are compatible and incompatible varieties, and in many cases though one variety (A) will pollinate another (B), it is found that (B) will not pollinate (A). Full and up-to-date lists that planters should consult are given in the leaflet " Fertility Rules in Fruit Planting " (John Innes Leaflet No. 4), which intending commercial planters should study. We give here, however, selections of good varieties and other information which will help the planter of a home fruit garden.

APPLES

Variety.	Flowering.	Date to pick.	To use.	Other remarks.
D. Allington Pippin	M.	Early Sept.	To Dec.	Good pollinator.
D. Blenheim Orange	M.	Mid-Oct.	To Jan.	Poor pollinator, does not fruit well until rather old.
Bramley's Seedling Crimson Bramley similar to Bramley	M.	Mid-Oct.	To March	Poor pollinator.
D. Beauty of Bath	E.	Early Aug.	Aug.	Good pollinator.
Crawley Beauty	L. (latest of all)	Late Oct.	To Feb.	Good pollinator.
D. Cox's Orange Pippin	M.	Early Oct.	To March	Good pollinator.
D. Ellison's Orange	M.	Late Sept.	To Oct.	Good pollinator. Succeeds where Cox's fails.
D. Lady Sudeley	M.	Late Aug.	Aug.–Sept.	Good flavour, good pollinator.
D. Laxton's Superb	M.	Oct.	To March	Good pollinator.

D. = dessert.
M. = midseason.
E. = early.
L. = late.

Note that a good pollinator will only cross-pollinate a variety that blooms at the same time.

PEARS

Variety.	Flowering.	Date to pick.	To use.	Other remarks.
Beurre D'Amanlis	E.	End Aug.	Early Sept.	Poor pollinator. Plant Louise Bonne as a pollinator.
Catillac	M.	Late Oct.	Feb.–April	Culinary pear. Poor pollinator.
Conference	E.	End Sept.	To Nov.	Good pollinator.
Laxton's Superb	M.	End Aug.	Early Sept.	Good pollinator.
Williams Bon Chretien	M.	End Aug.	Sept.	Good pollinator.
Louise Bonne	E.	Late Sept.	Oct.	Good pollinator.
Doyenne du Domice	L.	Early Oct.	Nov.	Good pollinator.

CHERRIES

Variety.	Flowering.	Date to pick.	Other remarks.
Black Eagle	M.	July	Waterloo would pollinate.
Frogmore Early	L.	End June	Kentish Bigarreau or Elton Heart would pollinate.
Bigarreau Napoleon	L.	Aug.	Frogmore Early and Kentish Bigarreau would pollinate.
Kentish Bigarreau	L.	Mid-July	Frogmore Early would pollinate.
Elton Heart	L.	Early July	Kentish Bigarreau would pollinate.
Waterloo	M.	Late June	Black Eagle would pollinate.

Morello and Kentish Red cherries will fruit well as isolated specimens.

N.B.—Where a cherry exists and is not at present fruiting well, if the variety is not known, choose one of these to plant as a companion—" Florence " or " Noble ". They flower late and will pollinate any other variety of cherry.

PLUMS

Variety	Flowering.	Gather.	Other remarks.
Cambridge Gage	L.	Mid-Aug.	Needs a pollinator, such as Czar or Pershore.
Pond's Seedling	L.	Sept.	Needs a pollinator, Czar or Per shore.
Purple Pershore	L.	Aug.	Will fruit in isolation.
Diamond	E.	Early Sept.	Needs pollinator such as Monarch
Late Orange	M.	Late Sept.	Needs pollinator such as Blaisdon Red.
Czar	L.	Mid-Aug.	Will fruit in isolation.
Victoria	M.	Mid-Aug.	Will fruit in isolation.

Note that the above are short lists only. Fuller lists should be consulted where large fruit orchards are planned.

SELF-FERTILITY

In every case there are some varieties which will fruit reasonably well without any companion tree, but *in most cases, with most fruits,* it is worth while to plant two varieties, as cross-pollination improves the crops even on so-called self-fertile fruits.

(*See also Note on the "Family Tree" on page 151.*)

CHAPTER XI

VEGETABLES AND SALADS

THE best way to teach yourself vegetable gardening is to divide the vegetables into groups according to the method of cultivation. To begin with, there are the "small-seed" crops—that is, crops that are grown from small seeds that are sown either on the main vegetable plot, or in a nursery bed to be transplanted when they are fit for the move. The seeds are sown on prepared soil, as described in Chapter VIII, the general method being to sow the seed in parallel lines running as nearly as possible north and south across the plot. To aid in regular sowing, a line of string is used, stretched across the plot between two short wooden posts or pegs. For small seeds a drill is drawn: this is a V-shaped trench, about 1 inch deep, drawn usually with a V-shaped hoe or the corner of a rake. It is best to move the line and draw a second drill before actually sowing the seed in the first row. The seed can then be sown thinly along the drill and lightly covered with soil. The rake jumped up and down along the row is generally an easy way to cover the seed with soil, and a last-minute rake between the rows each time the line is moved will obliterate footmarks and leave the plot tidy. A small label should stand at each end of each row of seed, partly to indicate the variety and date of each sowing, but partly so that when the first hoeing between the rows is done, the line can again be stretched in position as at first. This acts as a guide, and prevents many accidents. Nothing is more disconcerting than to find one is hoeing up the seedlings instead of merely the weeds!

Thinning of crops sown *in situ* must be done immediately the second leaves appear, and at this stage thinning should generally be such as to leave the seedlings 4 or 5 inches apart. A second thinning is desirable with most crops. Onions, carrots, lettuces and other crops that can be used very young are sometimes only thinned as required for use, but this is possible only when very careful, thin sowing has been done.

Regular use of the hoe as the crops develop is important: hoeing keeps the surface soil aerated and moist; it destroys weeds, and helps to keep away pests.

Certain vegetables are grown in double or treble rows. Broad beans and peas, for instance, are sown in this manner. A good method with peas is to take out a shallow trench, 3 or 4 inches deep, and the width of the spade-blade. In this trench-bottom the seeds are sown in three lines, 3 or 4 inches apart. Pea-sticks set at each side of the row after the seeds have been covered with 2 inches of good soil serve the double purpose of breaking the winds and supporting the plants when they grow.

Some vegetables are always raised under glass or in a nursery plot and moved later to the open. It is usual to plant these out with the help of a dibber—a tool resembling a sawn-off spade handle, slightly sharpened at the end. With this a hole of desired depth can be made, and after the seedling is put in position (or held with its roots in the hole) the soil is levered against the roots with the same tool. In a little garden a trowel can with advantage take the place of a dibber: it makes a better job of the planting, but takes a little longer.

Onions and shallots are sometimes grown from "sets"—*i.e.*, small bulbs which will increase in size or number when planted in the open. In these cases all that is needed is for the bulb to be pressed half-way into the soil. A firm bed of well-prepared soil is essential, and newly dug soil should be well trodden and raked before either onions or shallots are put out.

Potatoes are a type of vegetable that are not grown from seed in the garden, but from small tubers (these are, of course, called " seed potatoes "). For potatoes, a drill similar to that made for small seeds, but deep enough to allow for 4 or 5 inches of soil over each tuber, should be dug or drawn with a spade or pointed hoe. Potatoes should be started into new growth before planting time: for this the tubers are set " rose " end up in trays, in a light, warm place. If left in the dark, thin, weak stems will develop, but if in the light, short, dark green sprouts only will appear. Plant carefully, covering the tubers at once with soft soil and being careful not to damage the young shoots. If young new growth appears above the soil before the frosts are safely past, they may be damaged, so it is advisable to protect them at once, either by drawing soil up over them, or by using straw or bracken. Keep the hoe going to destroy weeds between the rows, and gradually earth up the potatoes by drawing soil up against the plant stems, until about 6 inches of soil has been so banked up along each side of the row. Reason: to prevent tubers turning green.

BLANCHING

Certain vegetables are unpalatable unless they are blanched—that is, made white (or NOT GREEN)—by the exclusion of light. Celery and leeks are blanched in the open: soil is drawn up against the plants, as in the case of potatoes, or paper collars are tied carefully round the stems, to exclude light. Chicory and sea-kale are more often blanched under cover, chiefly because they need both warmth and darkness to induce fresh growth. In these cases the old green tops are cut away, and the roots, lifted from the open ground, are replanted, or packed close together in deep boxes of soil. Fresh growth begins, and in order to keep this white and palatable, no light is allowed to reach it. A box deep enough to allow for a few inches of sand over the crowns of the plants can be used, and when the top growth appears above the sand, the crop is ready for use. Chicory is cut off without any part of the old root, but in the case of sea-kale, a tiny part of the old root is cut with the blanched top.

FIG. 61.—Two methods of blanching endive.

(a) A large flower-pot is inverted over a plant which is tied up previously.

(b) A tile is placed over the heart of the plant.

Roughly it takes about six weeks to force roots into blanched growth in this way (depending, of course, a little on the amount of warmth provided). Blanching of celery and leeks is done in successive stages, and is spread usually over six or eight weeks.

The following brief hints are designed to assist the student to apply general gardening principles to vegetable production. Reference should be made to other chapters for information *re* treatment of pests, soil preparation, harvesting, etc., and particularly to Chapters III and XII for suggestions as to the lay-out of a vegetable garden.

POPULAR VEGETABLE CROPS AND THEIR CULTIVATION

ARTICHOKES

Artichokes are of several kinds. **Jerusalem Artichokes** are a root crop, of which the tops grow tall and resemble giant sunflowers. They make a good windbreak if planted along the side of an exposed plot. Plant the tubers 15 inches apart and 6 inches deep in February. In good ground the tubers will each provide two or three pounds of artichokes, which can be lifted during the winter as required. Enough good-shaped tubers of medium size should be selected from each crop to re-plant in the next season.

Globe Artichokes are ornamental plants, of which the unopened flower-bud is used. They will only grow well in very rich soil, and they are not over-hardy, so that in many gardens a straw covering over the crowns is needed in winter.

Chinese Artichokes are somewhat similar to Jerusalem artichokes, and cultivated in the same way, except that the tubers can be set only 12 inches apart in rows, with 12 inches between the rows.

ASPARAGUS

Asparagus is a perennial, and a well-made asparagus bed will last twenty-five years. On clay soil the ground should be made up with a good quantity of burnt rubbish and leaf-mould. When well manured, and dug, it should be made into beds 5 feet wide, with alleys between the beds 2 feet wide. Roots can be bought, but if they have been raised from seed they can be moved to permanent positions when a year old. Set them in three rows in each 5-foot bed, with 2 inches of soil over the crowns. Allow 2 feet between the plants in the rows. Hoe in summer, use a mulch of old stable manure and soil in January, and a little nitrate of soda or liquid manure in May each year. Do not cut stems later than mid-June, and do not cut any until the plants have been in for more than twelve months. Each autumn cut down the tops and clear away all weeds from the beds.

BEANS

Broad Beans are sown in November, February or March, according to the type of soil and local conditions. Autumn sowing is best on light, sandy soil. Sow in double rows, 3 inches deep and 8 inches apart, with 2 feet between each pair of rows. Pinch out the tops when several flowers have formed: this not only encourages the swelling of the pods, but discourages the Black Fly, which attacks the tender growing tips.

Dwarf Beans. Sow these in May, in drills 18 inches apart and 2 inches deep. Thin to 1 foot apart, or sow one seed every 12 inches, with a few extra at one end of the row which can be used to fill up gaps. Gather regularly while young and tender.

Runner Beans. Sow in May, 3 inches deep, 6 inches apart, in double rows. Set bean poles in position for support, or, if poles cannot be used, pick out the growing tip of the plant when it begins to " run ", and again pick out the tips when the new side-growths run. This removal of the tips will create bushy dwarf plants. Gather pods young: if they begin to mature, plants will cease to flower. Guard against slugs while plants are young, and against aphis later. Use plenty of water, over the foliage and flowers, in dry spells.

Winter Beans. Sow as dwarf beans, but leave unpicked until mid-September. If bean pods are not yet ripe at that time, pull the whole plants and hang in small bunches, upside down, in a position where they will dry out. Shell and store when dry.

BEETROOT

Sow in drills 1 inch deep, drawn 15 inches apart. Thin to 1 foot apart in the rows—no transplanting. Sow for succession, a few in sheltered positions in April, main crop in May and June, and a further sowing of round beet in July if early crops do not come up to expectation.

Lift and store beet before the frosts, packing the roots in soil or sand, or piling them into a heap and covering with soil and straw.

BRASSICAS

Brassica is the family name of the greens—cabbage and savoys, sprouts, cauliflower, broccoli, and kale.

Cabbages are sown in spring, i.e. during the last half of April, on a prepared seed-bed, transplanted as the ground and the seedlings become ready in June or July, to mature for use in late summer and autumn. They are sown again in May or June, transplanted in July or August, for late winter use. And again they are sown at the end of July in the north and the first week in August in the south, for transplanting mid-September to mid-October, this last sowing to produce spring greens (i.e. alternate plants, immature) in March and good-hearted cabbages in spring and early summer. Thus, by sowing at three seasons, a continuous supply of cabbage is produced all the year round. Set out cabbage plants 2 feet apart each way on ground that has been well manured and dressed with garden lime. Summer-sown cabbages can be set rather closer in the rows, as alternate plants will be pulled for spring greens in March. When planting cabbages on dry ground, make a hole for each seedling, fill this with water, and plant when the water has soaked away. With a start in life of this kind, cabbages are not likely to run to seed.

Savoys should be sown in May, and planted out in July or August on ground manured for a previous crop. Hoe in 2 oz. of superphosphate and 1 oz. of potash salts per square yard (or some bonfire ash) before planting. Savoys are harvested after the first frosts.

Sprouts should be sown in late March or early April. Transplant 2 feet apart each way in May or June, during showery weather. Remove yellow leaves in autumn. Gather sprouts from the bottom first.

Cauliflower is sown in April and transplanted, 18 inches apart each way, at the end of May. Dress the ground with a light dusting of superphosphate before planting. Sulphate of ammonia or nitrate of soda used as a liquid stimulant will speed up growth.

Broccoli is sown as cauliflower, and transplanted in June or July, as the ground becomes vacant. It is best planted out on ground manured for a previous crop, but only hoed on the surface, i.e. not recently disturbed to any great depth. Two ounces of superphosphate, with some bonfire ash, to each square yard, before sowing or planting, will produce plants that can stand the winter. This applies both to the white-headed and purple sprouting types.

Kale. Sow during May in a seed-bed, and transplant in July or August, 2 feet apart each way, except the variety "Hungry Gap", which is best sown in early July where it is to mature, and thinned later to 18 inches apart each way.

CARROTS

Grow these just as advised for beet, except that earlier and later sowings can be made for the production of small tender roots.

CELERIAC

Sow and plant out as celery, but not in trenches. Instead of earthing up, draw the soil a little away from the plants a few weeks before they are ready. Use roots from the ground, or lift and store in November.

CELERY

Sow the seed in boxes under glass in March. Prick out, and grow on without check. Meanwhile prepare trenches 15 inches wide and 1 foot deep. Fork in manure or compost in the trench bottom, then return some of the soil, leaving the trench 3 inches lower than the original soil level, with the ridges flattened between the trenches. On these flat ridges small salad crops can be grown. Plant the celery seedlings at the end of May or in June, in staggered rows, allowing 10 or 12 inches from plant to plant. When the plants are 15 inches high, begin to earth up. Draw a little moist soil from the sides up against the plants, which can, if desired, be tied round just under the foliage with raffia, or, alternatively, they can have stiff paper "collars" tied round the stems to protect them. After three weeks draw a little more soil up, and repeat this after a further three weeks, finally banking soil firmly up to the base of the foliage, so that only green tips are visible.

CHICORY

Sow and grow like lettuce, but in November lift the roots, trim away the tops, and force into new growth as described earlier in this chapter.

CUCUMBER

Outdoor cucumbers are raised under glass like marrows, and the plants can be set out, when all danger of frost is past, either in well-manured ground on the vegetable plot, or prepared " ridges ". Ridges are banks of manure and soil mixed, built to a ridge shape, so that more plants can be accommodated than on the flat. Allow plenty of water, and gather fruits when still small and tender. A fruit that bulges in one place, or is hard and yellow, is almost useless.

EGG PLANTS

Egg plants are so called because the fruits sometimes resemble eggs: sometimes, however, they are long and purple. Seeds are sown like tomatoes under glass, and the plants set out in ground prepared as for tomatoes. No stopping or training is needed, but plenty of sunshine is essential.

LEEKS

Sow in the soil of the frame or under cloches in February. When planting out in summer, merely make a deep hole with a dibber and drop in one plant; afterwards water well, and some of the soil from the sides will wash down sufficiently to make the roots firm in the ground. It is not wise to plant out leek seedlings until they are about 1 foot or more high: if they are sown thinly they should not suffer in the seed-bed through being left long enough to get to this height. Dig leeks for use as required.

LETTUCE

Sow thinly in drills 1 inch deep and 1 foot apart, and thin to 1 foot apart, using the thinnings for soups and salads or transplanting them where desired. Lettuces can be used to fill up spaces between tall or slow-growing crops. Sulphate of ammonia or nitrate of soda, a pinch to each seedling, will speed up growth if water is also given. Sow lettuces every three or four weeks from March until September, for continuous supplies. Protect the latest sowing with cloches in winter.

ENDIVE

Sow in June as lettuce, and in July and August sow the Batavian type in the same way. Blanch as required, when the plants are well grown (see diagram). It takes three weeks at least for blanching to be perfect.

MARROWS

Sow in pots under glass in March, and move to the open when all danger of frost is over. Or, if preferred. sow direct on a well-manured patch of ground, three seeds in a group, in the last half of April, and protect the seedlings with a handglass until the frosts are past, Copious water and sunshine are needed. Cut marrows when they are still young and tender: they are better for cooking, and more marrows will be produced.

ONIONS

Sow in boxes under glass in February, or sow outdoors later in a nursery plot, or where they are to mature. If preferred, sow in August and leave the onions in the seed-rows until spring, planting them out in early March, or thinning them where they stand, to leave them 6 to 8 inches apart in the rows, with 1 foot between the rows. Feed with nitrate of soda or sulphate of ammonia every three weeks during summer (1 oz. in 1 gal. of water). Bend over the tops in mid-August, to speed up ripening of the bulbs. Lift at the end of the month and store in a dry cool place where air can circulate round the bulbs.

PARSNIPS

Sow in February or early March, in drills 1 inch deep, 15 inches apart. Thin to 1 foot apart in the rows. Lift after the first touch of frost, or dig as required. Parsnips prefer ground that has not been recently manured, but is in good heart. If grown on stony ground, make large holes with a dibber, and fill them with prepared sifted compost: sow the seeds three or four on each site, and thin to one strong seedling.

PEAS

Well manure the ground, and dust lime over the surface. Take out a shallow trench, about 10 inches wide and 3 inches deep. Sow the peas in this, spacing them 2 or 3 inches apart over the shallow trench; cover with 2 or 3 inches of soil and press this down. Set pea-sticks in position at once. Peas can be sown for succession at intervals from February until late June.

Sugar peas are grown exactly as ordinary garden peas, but the pods are gathered and cooked whole before the peas develop inside (as runner beans).

POTATOES

" Early ", " second early " and " main crop " potatoes are offered by seedsmen. Only the early and second early are grown in most small gardens, as main-crop potatoes can be raised more economically on farms. Buy tubers (" seed potatoes ") in January and set them immediately to sprout, rose end uppermost, in shallow trays. Light and freedom from frost are essential during the sprouting period. Plant them out from late March to late April, according to the weather and soil conditions, allowing 1 foot from tuber to tuber in the rows and 18 inches between the rows of early potatoes, and more space for the later crops. Potatoes are a useful crop for cleaning newly broken grassland: the crop grown on such land will probably be attacked by wireworm and other pests, but if it is lifted and used early in the winter, this will remove from the soil a great many unwanted pests!

It has already been stated above that potatoes should be earthed up as they are hoed. This is not an essential practice, and is not done on all farms, where it is thought that the labour involved is more than the results are worth. There is, in fact, a section of the gardening community who claim that such hoeing disturbs the roots of the potatoes and so does more harm than good. So it may be taken that where weeds are not troublesome, much hoeing can be dispensed with, but where weeds have to be tackled, hoeing (with some discretion) is probably an advantage. When the tops begin to yellow, potatoes are lifted for storage: they must not remain in the ground too long, for if the weather is fine and warm they may begin to grow again from the new tubers, while if frosts occur, the tubers will be useless. The best way to store large quantities of potatoes is in a clamp outdoors, i.e. a heap of tubers piled on to a straw bed, with straw and soil to cover them, so as to exclude frost. All main-crop potatoes should be sprayed with Bordeaux mixture in June, early July and mid-July, to prevent "Blight"; otherwise they will not keep well in store.

SHALLOTS

Plant in February. "Sets" are used, and these are pressed fully half-way into the soil. Allow 8 inches between sets in the row and 1 foot between rows. Lift in July, when the foliage yellows, and store as onions. Select a few medium-sized sound bulbs for replanting the next season. **Garlic** is grown in the same way.

SPINACH

Several kinds of spinach are in common cultivation. **Summer Spinach** and **Winter Spinach** are sown and grown like lettuce, a few leaves being gathered from each plant as required. Both are hardy, and will stand mild winters in the open.

Perpetual Spinach, or spinach beet, is a beet of which the leaves can be used like spinach, though the roots become tough and useless. This, too, is hardy, and can be cut in winter and spring. Plants should be thinned to stand 18 inches apart.

" **Orache** " is another " spinach " that can be grown from seed sown in spring. The plants grow from 3 to 5 feet high, and the youngest tender leaves are gathered for use.

Sea-Kale Beet or **Silver Beet** is yet another substitute for spinach. In this case the seeds are sown on the plot, as summer spinach, and thinned to about 1 foot apart. Both the green part of the leaf (as spinach) and the silvery stem and midrib (as sea kale) are eaten, hence the name Seakale Beet. This vegetable should be sown annually in March, but old plants that stand the winter need not be discarded too hurriedly, as they send up fresh leaves which are very useful at times in the spring.

SWEET CORN

Sow under glass in April and plant out 12 inches apart at end of May. Or sow outdoors in May. Gather cobs while still *milky*.

TOMATOES

For outdoor culture tomatoes are sown under glass in early spring, pricked out, as soon as the rough leaves show, into single pots, or into deep boxes, and grown on until the end of May, when they are fit to put into the garden. Amateur gardeners who have no heat in the greenhouse are advised to buy plants, and to choose those which appear thick and short-stemmed, with dark-coloured foliage, for these are well grown, and hardened off properly. Plant out 18 inches apart in soil dressed with bonemeal or superphosphate and wood ash. Tie immediately to stakes, and pinch out side stems as they appear, limiting each plant to a single cane, on which five or six trusses of fruit and flowers should develop by the second week in August. Then pinch out the tip of the plant, to allow all the food to go into the swelling fruits, and at the same time spray the plants with Bordeaux Mixture, to prevent the appearance of Blight.

TURNIPS AND SWEDES

Turnips and swedes must be sown where they are to mature, and not transplanted. Dress the ground with superphosphate before sowing, and hoe this in well. Then sow in drills 15 inches apart. Thin to leave the plants 1 foot apart. Turnips can be sown every three weeks from April to early July. Swedes should be sown in May or early June. Early sowings are often attacked by the flea beetle, and daily dustings with Derris, after spraying with water, are useful. Harvest turnips when no larger than tennis balls, and swedes when scarcely any larger. Store for winter in the same way as carrots.

RHUBARB

This is generally grown in the vegetable garden. It can be planted in spring in rich soil. Do not pull any stems for twelve months after planting. To force rhubarb easily, invert a deep box over it and pack straw round the sides. Do this in December for early supplies.

HERBS

Herbs grown for use in the kitchen must form a part of any home vegetable garden. These culinary herbs divide themselves naturally into two groups—those best raised from seed and those grown commonly from roots or cuttings.

Herbs grown from seed are sown usually in rows 1 foot apart in a special herb plot. It is, however, possible to make a decorative feature of a herb garden, and in that case the perennial herbs may form the permanent backbone of the garden, and the annual herbs, or those grown from seed each season, can be sown in irregular groups to fit in with the planting scheme.

Popular Garden Herbs

Name.	Sow in.	Plant.	Remarks.
Chives . .	—	March or Oct.	Lift and divide every third year.
Fennel . .	April	March	Divide old roots in March.
Horse-radish .	—	Autumn or winter	Increase by cutting of crowns.
Marjoram .	March	Spring or autumn	Divide old roots in March or Oct.
Parsley . .	March and July	—	Discard old roots each season.
Sage . .	—	Spring or autumn	Take cuttings in April.
Summer Savory	April	—	—
Winter Savory.	—	March	Divide old roots in March.
Tarragon. .	—	March	Divide old roots in March.
Thyme . .	March	April	Take cuttings in summer.

No special treatment is needed for herbs. The annuals are sown thinly, broadcast or in rows, and thinned out to allow sufficient room for full development.

Cuttings are taken either in late spring or early summer, or sometimes in August, of such subjects as sage, rosemary and thyme. Horse-radish is increased by cutting off " crowns " with pieces of root about 2 inches long, and replanting these in good soil in February. After nearly two years they will have made roots thick enough to use in the kitchen. Chives are increased by dividing the clumps. Mint is increased by division of the roots during winter. Mint easily becomes a " weed ", and so does horse-radish, and for this reason they are often grown in small beds where they cannot encroach on other herbs. Mint does very well in a damp, shady situation, whereas most herbs are of better flavour if grown in full sun.

DIARY OF THE VEGETABLE PLOT

January

Decide on cropping plans. Order seeds. Prepare frames, hotbeds, cloches, seed boxes and pots.

Sort over tools, insecticides, fertilizers, and order fresh supplies where needed.

Sow in heated frames or greenhouses: tomato, lettuce, radish, cucumbers and early carrots. Where no heat is available, wait for warmer days before sowing.

Plant horse-radish.

Force seakale, chicory, rhubarb.

Set potatoes to sprout.

February

Where soil is rather poor, dust a little general garden fertilizer over the soil in preparing seed beds.

Sow over hotbed, or in frames where frosts can be excluded, leeks, onions, lettuce, cauliflower and small salads.

Sow in the open parsnips, broad beans, a few early peas and in sheltered plots a few cabbages and spinach.

Plant a few early potatoes, shallots, garlic and Jerusalem artichokes. Lift and divide chives.

March

Prepare nursery seed beds and tread and rake the rows on the main vegetable plots in preparation for main sowings.

Sow in the nursery beds cabbage, savoy, sprouts, cauliflower (if not sown under glass), broccoli, lettuce.

Sow in heat celery, celeriac, aubergine (egg plant).

Sow in the open garden peas, carrots, parsley, radish, turnips, spinach, onions, lettuce.

Plant early potatoes. Plant out onions.

Make new herb gardens. Renovate old herb beds and prepare for seed sowing.

April

Hoe between rows of seedlings and thin out seedlings where necessary at the earliest possible opportunity.

Sow on the plot: Beet (except in very cold districts), carrots, turnips, peas, spinach, salads and herbs.

Sow runner and dwarf beans at the end of the month in warm gardens.

Harden off seedlings under glass, before planting out.

Make celery trenches.

Dust calomel dust among onion seedlings, and naphthalene among carrot seedlings to ward off pests.

Plant potatoes.

May

Finish potato planting if not already done.

Sow french and runner beans, peas, turnips, kale, beet, and salads.

Sow marrows and cucumbers outdoors if good rich soil can be provided and cloches used to protect the seedlings. Otherwise buy plants at the end of the month, if they have not been raised under glass.

June

Finish all planting out of seedlings raised under glass. Hoe regularly. Cease cutting asparagus in the middle of the month.

Sow salads, peas (for succession), swedes, carrots, endive, chicory.

Plant tomatoes, marrows, melons (in frames), cucumbers, cabbage, sprouts, broccoli, leeks.

Spray main-crop potatoes.

July

Lift early potatoes, and immediately rake over the vacant ground and plant out winter greens of all kinds.

Sow turnips, beet, carrots, salads and winter spinach.

Plant celery in trenches, celeriac, broccoli, kales.

Gather and dry herbs for winter use.

Spray main-crop potatoes.

August

Continue to plant out kale and savoys.

Bend over onion tops to encourage ripening of the bulbs. Spray tomatoes in the second week of the month.

Sow cabbage, onions, lettuce, turnips, radishes.

September

Sow spinach for winter. Sow lettuce and protect the seed rows with cloches.

Plant cabbage at the end of the month.

Earth up celery and leeks. Store onions. Set out lettuce seedlings in frames for the winter.

October

Sow cauliflower to winter in frames, and lettuce also if they were not set out last month.

Lift and store root crops and begin to force chicory, rhubarb, seakale.

November

Sow broad beans.

Begin to double dig vacant ground. Use soil fumigant during digging if required.

Clear rubbish, dead plant tops, leaves etc., and build them into a compost heap. Dig in the material from the old compost heap during trenching. Burn woody rubbish and diseased plants.

December

Double dig and manure vacant ground. Begin to make up hotbeds if fresh manure is available. Use garden lime over beds in the kitchen garden, after digging.

Force chicory, seakale and rhubarb as needed.

CHAPTER XII

INTENSIVE CULTIVATION

INTENSIVE cultivation merely means that every square foot of soil available is used, and that it is used to the full—that is, at every season of the year the ground is occupied and producing a crop of some kind, and as fast as one crop is gathered, the soil is taken over by some other crop. This succession of crops is based on the time in which the different kinds of vegetables reach maturity and on their hardiness and season.

Where French gardening is practised, the full use of the soil is made possible by building up hotbeds, so that early and late crops are encouraged, and by well-devised systems of irrigation, so that summer drought does not interfere with the growth of a crop. An experienced gardener can gradually introduce methods of this kind into his schemes, but in view of the differences in climate, it is not possible to work, in Britain, on exactly the same systems as in France. We shall therefore merely glance at the general principles of intensive culture, and leave the gardener to work out his own system from these.

Some crops take extra large quantities of particular plant-foods from the soil: brassicas take a good deal of nitrate, while tomatoes take phosphates, and roots generally take an excess of potash. Because of such differences, we plan our vegetable gardens to allow for rotation of crops. We may divide the plot into three and grow greens in one, roots in another, and legumes (peas and beans), tomatoes, onions, and other "odds" in the third portion. Or, if needed, we may grow potatoes in a fourth plot. In either case we can economise in the use of fertilisers by moving our crops on to the next plot each year. Heavy compost manuring for the tomatoes and other " odds " one season, followed by the use of artificial fertilisers in the next year for root-

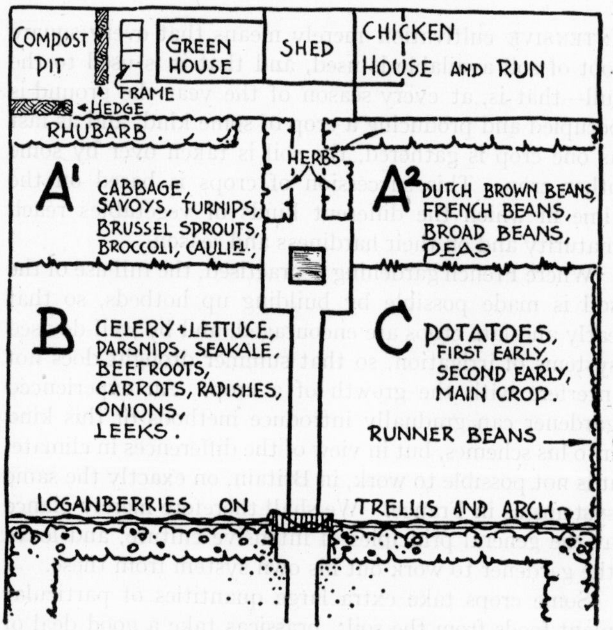

FIG. 62.—System of crop rotation.

To cultivate land intensively, a system of rotation must be strictly followed, as shown in the above plan.

crops, and lime in the third season for the greens, will keep both plot and plants in good condition.

In adopting a system of real intensive culture, however, we have not only to plan for rotation in this way, we have to see that every plot is fully occupied all the time.

This is done in two ways. In the early part of the year some crops that will remain on the plot all the season are still quite small, and do not fully occupy the site allocated to them. So, during this early season, seeds of some quick-growing crop, such as radishes, spinach and cress, are sown between rows of the main crop, and these mature in time to be cleared away before the other plants need the extra space. Then, again, when a quick-to-mature, early crop (say of peas) is cleared, a second crop is immediately sown. In some cases, the follow-on crop is actually sown or planted before the first crop is harvested: in the case of potatoes, for instance, seedlings of winter greens may be set out between the rows immediately the potatoes have been earthed up. In this way the follow-on crop becomes well settled in the soil and able to occupy the ground very quickly when the potatoes have been dug.

Now and again it becomes desirable to leave a plot of soil vacant for a time, or to sow it with mustard in order to "green manure" it, the mustard plants being dug into the soil when convenient, but before they have reached flowering stage. Every gardener must make plans of this kind to suit his particular plot, his family requirements and his local conditions. The following table is therefore given as a guide to the gardening student, in order that he may work out a system of inter-cropping. A word or two of warning: intensive cultivation is only possible where soil can be kept reasonably fertile, warm and moist at all seasons. Intensive cultivation does not mean crowding—it implies that at all times plants shall be allowed enough, but not too much room for development. Lastly, intensive cultivation demands constant attention on the part of the cultivator, and pests, diseases, starvation and delays must all be fought if the system is to be a success.

TIMING TABLE FOR VEGETABLES AND SALADS

Crop.	Time of germination of seed (approx.).	Time to mature after sowing or or planting.
Artichokes, tuberous	—	30 weeks
Asparagus	2–3 weeks	2–3 years
Broad beans	14 days	15 weeks
Dwarf beans	14 days	3 months
Runner beans	14 days	15 weeks
Winter beans	14 days	4 months
Broccoli	10 days	5–6 months
Brussels sprouts	10 days	6 months
Beetroot	2–3 weeks	4 months
Cabbages	10 days	18 weeks
Carrots	2–3 weeks	5 months
Cauliflower	10 days	5 months
Celeriac	15 days	6 months
Celery	15 days	6–7 months
Chicory	1–2 weeks	6 months
Colewort	10 days	5–6 months
Corn salad	9 days	2–3 months
Cress (garden)	5 days	10 days
Cress (land)	10 days	2 months
Cucumber, ridge	1–2 weeks	4–5 months
Endive	1–2 weeks	16 weeks
Kale	8 days	5–10 months
Kohl rabi	1–2 weeks	7 months
Leeks	1–2 weeks	6–7 months
Lettuce	6–10 days	10 weeks
Mustard	4 days	9 days
Onions	10 days	7 months
Parsnip	2–3 weeks	8 months
Peas	1–2 weeks	3–4 months
Potatoes	—	16 weeks or more, according to variety, etc.
Radish	1 week	7 weeks
Savoy	5–10 days	5–6 months
Seakale	2–3 weeks	21 months
Shallots	—	25 weeks
Spinach	10 days	12 weeks
Swede	12 days	7 months
Tomato	1–2 weeks	3–4 months
Turnips	1–2 weeks	12 weeks
Vegetable marrows	1–2 weeks	12 weeks

Note that these are all approximate times, as much depends on conditions of heat and moisture.

CHAPTER XIII

PESTS AND DISEASES

PERHAPS the most difficult of all gardening knowledge to teach yourself is knowledge about pests and diseases. Full knowledge is an ideal not obtained even by the expert, for every year adds to our discoveries in this wide field of research. Knowledge on general lines can, however, be acquired quite simply if the subject is approached on the following lines:—

In the case of pests, these fall naturally into groups. There are **soil pests,** living below the surface and damaging the plants generally by attacks on their roots. The most common are:—

Wireworms. About 1 inch long and $\frac{1}{12}$ inch thick, wiry in texture and worm-like in appearance, of a light yellowish-brown colour. They are numerous in newly dug pastures, and gradually disappear with good cultivation.

Cutworms. Longer than wireworms, and more than $\frac{1}{4}$ inch thick; like large underground caterpillars, whitish, or a sickly greyish-green colour.

Leatherjackets. Usually shorter than wireworms and with fat bodies, generally matching the soil in colour, or slaty brown, and very tough-skinned. Chickens refuse them, but some birds will tackle them. Found frequently eating through grass roots, and so making lawns brown and bare in patches.

Millipedes. When at rest these coil round like tight, flat "springs". They are slaty in colour, and have many legs. Centipedes, which are golden yellow or brown and have fewer legs, run fast, and do not coil up, are not harmful to plants.

These soil pests and others are difficult to control. Hand-picking during winter digging helps, and where soil fumigant can be used the numbers will be reduced. Soil fumigant is sold by sundriesmen, and destroys pests by fumes that rise through the soil. It must therefore

FIG. 63.—Careful spraying, wetting the undersides of the leaves as well as the tops, is the treatment for most pests in summer.

be put well down below the top spit, as advised by the makers.

Another group of pests is called " **sucking insects** ". This includes various-coloured aphis (black fly, green fly, etc.), woolly aphis, which resembles cotton-wool and is found on the bark of trees, and the well-known frog-hopper or cuckoo-spit. All these are controlled by contact sprays, except the woolly aphis, and in this case the cotton-wool protective covering keeps contact sprays away from the pest itself. Where woolly aphis is seen, it should be dabbed with methylated spirit, the operation being done with a small brush and repeated when necessary until the pest disappears.

Biting pests are a third group. These include the various caterpillars and sawflies, beetles, etc. A poisonous spray (or dust) on the surface of the foliage or stems that are attacked is needed to destroy the pests. Of poison sprays the best for general use are derris or pyrethrum compounds, for these can be used freely without harm to humans. Nicotine and arsenic sprays have at times to be resorted to, but in general it is best to use these only when other sprays fail.

The last group is what might be called the " hit and run " group. In this I should place the cabbage-root fly, the leaf-miners and the raspberry beetle. The cabbage-root fly, for instance, lays its eggs in the soil near seedling cabbages and other greens, and then disappears. It is the resulting maggot that eats through the root and damages the plant. Soil fumigants are useless, as they can only be effectively used in winter, when the fly is not there. Calomel dust used as a dressing over the soil when the flies are likely to be active is the modern solution of the problem, and this treatment also serves to keep down attacks of onion and carrot flies, which have more or less the same habit of attack.

Raspberry beetles appear when the flowers are open, and lay their eggs in the young fruits. Derris dusted or sprayed into the flowers or over the fruit trusses when the flowers have just faded will reduce the trouble to negligible proportions.

Leaf-miners are pests that can be prevented, rather than cured. The maggots that eat their way between the leaf surfaces, and leave tunnelling marks on them are the result of eggs laid by a fly. The use of a deterrent insecticide over the foliage in the early stages of growth will keep the fly away. Paraffin emulsion is good for this purpose, but some growers prefer to use a good commercial insecticide, as most of these contain deterrent, contact poison and food poison in the one spray, and so are useful against most of the summer pests.

Big bud is a pest that falls into none of the categories above. It is practically invisible to the naked eye, but its effect is visible enough, for the buds on the stems that ought to be pointed acquire a flat, round appearance when attacked by the mite, and they fail to develop properly. It has been found that spraying the bushes with lime-sulphur when the foliage is just about the size of a shilling is an effective control of the pest. This is a precaution that all black-currant growers should take, as the mite is not only harmful in itself, but is a carrier of disease.

DISEASES

Plant diseases are brought by insect carriers, and by infection through the soil, or by wind-blown spores alighting on open wounds. This suggests ways in which disease can be controlled. First by clean cultivation and rotation of crops, for if disease is carried from season to season in the soil, an obvious way to check it is by not providing in the second season a suitable plant medium for it. Thus, if club root appears, no brassicas of any kind should be grown in that particular plot for a few years and—a point that is often missed—no weeds of the same family should be allowed to grow. Charlock and wallflowers, for instance, are plants that might carry the infection over from year to year, as these plants are also liable to succumb to the disease.

Another way to fight disease is by the cultivation of strong plants, for these, like healthy, virile humans, are less liable to become victims of an epidemic. And finally, the immediate destruction of pests will help also to control diseases.

As with pests, diseases can be roughly grouped. There are diseases that result from weather conditions—that is, the diseases are more prevalent under certain conditions than others. Mildew is an illustration: one cannot avoid the presence of mildew, for the spores are everywhere; but by careful attention to ventilation and watering under glass, and by immediate spraying if the disease appears in the open, the gardener can prevent its spread. Green sulphur powder dusted over the plants or Bordeaux mixture sprayed on to them, are ways in which diseases such as mildew and the common "blight" of potatoes can be controlled or prevented. These diseases enter, or remain, on the plant surfaces, and so can be reached by sprays. There are certain diseases, however, that cannot be controlled by sprays or dusts, as the virus that is responsible is in the tissues of the plant. Reversion—the disease that turns black currants into "nettleheads" (that is, alters the bud formation, and renders the plant unproductive)—is an example of disease that cannot be controlled by spraying. There is, in fact, no remedy for the trouble, and affected plants have to be grubbed out and burnt. Fortunately the disease is not carried through the soil, and new plants can be put in at once to take the place of the old. Reversion is, however, believed to be carried by the big bud mite, so that destruction of this pest will have some bearing on the control of reversion.

On the whole, the best advice to a small garden owner with regard to diseases is that when an infected plant of any kind is seen, it should be destroyed, safety first being the motto. In larger plantations diseases are often too widespread to be treated in this cavalier fashion, and regular spraying is advisable to prevent wholesale losses.

Lack of space prevents detailed investigation of pests and diseases here, but the spraying calendar given below will assist the gardener to keep his plants healthy and trouble free.

LAWN PROBLEMS

Lawn troubles, apart from the work of leather-jackets mentioned above, are mainly concerned with the appearance of weeds. These can be treated in the obvious ways of hand-weeding, the use of the popular " walking-stick weed-killers ", which are tools that inject a portion of weed-killer into the heart of each large weed, and, best of all, digging up old, weedy turf and re-sowing the whole plot. There is, however, another—perhaps the most popular—method of dealing with lawns that have been allowed to become weedy—that is, with the use of lawn-sand or selective weed-killers.

These must not be confused with the ordinary weed-killers that are sold to destroy weeds on vacant plots. Sodium chlorate and arsenical weed-killers are designed to destroy every sort of living vegetation on a gravel path, but to use such chemicals on a lawn would obviously be fatal. Lawn-sand, on the other hand, is actually a fertiliser, but it is used to destroy the weed foliage by burning it off. The result is a partial blackening of the lawn for a week or two. Actually the foliage of weeds lies flatter than do the blades of fine grass, and they are more thickly covered by the sand, with the result that the weeds are burned more than the grass. The fertiliser in the lawn-sand then helps to stimulate growth of the grass, and so, as the lawn recovers, the weeds are crowded out by the grass. That is the theory of lawn-sand treatment, and it will be readily seen that such treatment may have to be repeated several times before it is completely effective.

Selective weed-killers are actually a form of growth-promoting substance. They act by causing abnormal growth of weeds, leading first to distortion and later to death. They affect most weeds, but do not harm the grass, and if used as recommended by the makers they are a wonderful help to the gardener.

CALENDAR OF PEST DESTRUCTION AND DISEASE CONTROL

January. Finish spraying with tar-oil and petroleum oil winter washes all fruit trees (not nuts) : this destroys eggs that have been laid in bark crevices.

February. Use Cheshunt compound as a soil drench in preparing potting-soil for seed-raising.

March. Apply weed-killer to gravel paths. At the end of March use lime-sulphur spray or Bordeaux mixture on pears, to control scab. Use lead arsenate spray if necessary to control caterpillars.

April. Use derris dust among vegetables to keep down all kinds of insect pests. Use lime-sulphur spray on apples (for scab) and black currants (for big bud).

May. Green fly is almost sure to appear this month on roses, chrysanthemums and on greenhouse plants: spray with any good insecticide, or dust with derris powder. Use lime-sulphur again (at petal fall) on apples.

June. Spray with insecticide to *prevent* as well as to control attacks of green and black fly. Use derris dust on raspberries and gooseberries, against beetles and sawflies. Use Bordeaux or Burgundy mixture on potatoes in the middle and end of the month, to prevent blight: careful spraying, to wet both sides of the leaves, is important.

July. Watch for mildew: green sulphur powder, or any commercial preparation for the purpose, should be used immediately the whitish powder is seen on roses, chrysanthemums, pot plants, etc. Spray potatoes a third time with Bordeaux or Burgundy mixture, to prevent blight. This spray is only necessary on the late crops intended for store.

August. Use derris dust among green vegetables to prevent attacks of fly or caterpillar. Spray tomatoes with Bordeaux mixture.

September. Apply grease-bands to fruit trees to catch the female (wingless) winter moth as she crawls up the trunk to lay her eggs near dormant buds. These bands can be bought in small quantities, ready greased. Clean up every patch of soil as the crops are harvested, and burn all diseased plant-tops. Put the remainder in the compost pit, where they will not encourage pests. Fumigate glasshouses if needed.

October. Watch for pests under glass, and keep outdoor plots very clean. Use worm-killer on lawns.

November. Hoe and clean up the surface soil among shrubs, fruits and other plants as possible: autumn cultivation allows birds to help in cleaning the soil. Use soil fumigant on land that is being trenched.

December. Begin spraying with tar-oil wash. Continue to trench, and use soil fumigant.

CHAPTER XIV

STORING VEGETABLES AND FRUIT

NOT every fruit and vegetable grown in the garden can be stored, though the great majority can be kept for use out of season, either by bottling, drying or storing.

As each needs some special consideration, let us deal with the most popular kinds alphabetically.

Artichokes. Globe artichokes—a summer crop—can only be used fresh. Jerusalem and Chinese artichokes can be left in the ground until required, or lifted after the frosts have cut down the tops, and stored in boxes of damp sand.

Beans are preserved by drying (either whole green pods or ripe seeds), bottling or salting.

Beetroots should be lifted when fully grown, the tops twisted off an inch or two above the roots, and the roots then stored in boxes of slightly damp sand, or in a clamp. A clamp is made as follows: a position as dry as possible is selected in the open, and a layer of straw laid down. Over this the roots are built into a pyramid or ridge-shaped heap. This also is covered with straw, which should, as far as possible, lie in similar manner to the thatch of a roof. Covering the straw must be 6 inches to 1 foot thickness of soil, beaten well so that it remains consolidated, to keep out frosts. Usually about 4 inches of straw and 6 inches of soil are needed. The soil used can be dug out immediately round the clamp, thus leaving a kind of moat which will assist in keeping the clamp dry. To enable surplus heat and moisture to escape, and so prevent trouble inside the clamp, a few wisps of straw are twisted loosely and inserted at the apex of the clamp, chimney-wise.

A clamp can be made in very similar manner inside a shed, but in this case only the bottom layer and covering of straw may be needed. The chief point to remember in storing roots is that, while frost must be excluded, a small amount of moisture and air among the roots is welcome. That is why roots store very well in boxes filled with slightly damp sand.

Carrots. Cut off the tops 2 inches above the roots and store as beetroots.

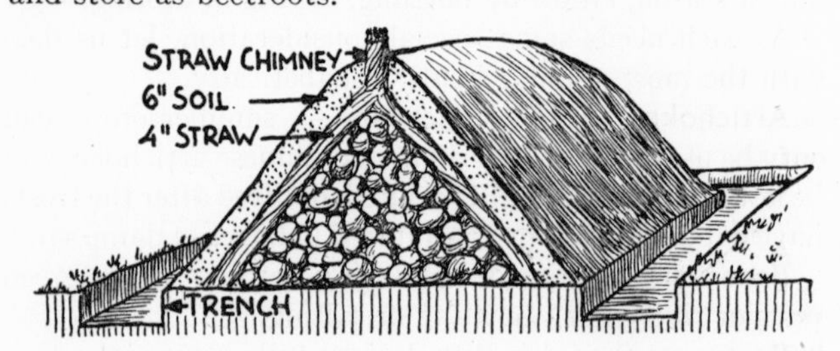

FIG. 64.—Simple method of storing potatoes.
Make a pie in the open garden : make a heap of the potatoes, cover with straw, and soil as shown above.

Cauliflowers are not stored for long periods, but if a number reach perfection at one time, they can be kept fresh for ten days by hanging them up by the roots in a cool, dark shed, or by trimming off some of the foliage and standing the heads close together, keeping them slightly damped over daily until they are used.

Celeriac. Store as beet.

Onions, Shallots and **Garlic** are all stored in much the same way. The bulbs, when fully grown, should be lifted, and then left to dry for a day or two before actually storing. They can be roped together, or just stored in any dry, cool shed until required.

Parsnips. Store like beet, or leave in the ground until required.

Potatoes are stored in clamps, as beetroot. The tubers should be carefully inspected before the clamp is made, and any diseased or damaged specimens must be taken out or the whole clamp may be affected. If potatoes that have been attacked by blight have to be stored, store them in small batches, and dust lime among the tubers. Inspect them frequently: blight causes an unpleasant odour to pervade the clamp, and when this is noticed, the clamp should be opened and the good tubers used at once.

Turnip. Store like beet: the only turnips left to winter in the open should be those of which the tops are to be eaten, as slow winter growth makes the roots tough.

Tomatoes picked green, but fully grown, will ripen indoors. The best way is to lay out the fruits in a single layer on trays, so that they can be frequently inspected. Tomatoes wrapped and packed together in boxes often turn out badly, as one diseased tomato will infect the whole crop.

FRUITS

Apples are stored either in special fruit cabinets, or trays, or in clamps. They should generally be turned out carefully from the picker's baskets on to a floor under cover and left a day or two before storing. Then store in a single layer, over straw, to prevent shrivelling, or make a clamp as described for storing beetroot indoors. A new preparation for dipping apples before storing is claimed to keep the late cooking-apples in better condition, and is worth a trial.

At the time of going to press, the experimental stage is not quite past, but the beneficial effect on certain varieties has already been proved.

Nuts. If cobnuts and similar nuts are to be stored, pack them into jars with layers of salt between, and tie them down with pieces of calico dipped in paraffin wax.

Pears. Store as apples, but keep an even sharper eye on the stored fruits, as pears quickly become " sleepy ".

It is worth mention that the usual storage temperature for all vegetables and fruits stored without salt or cooking

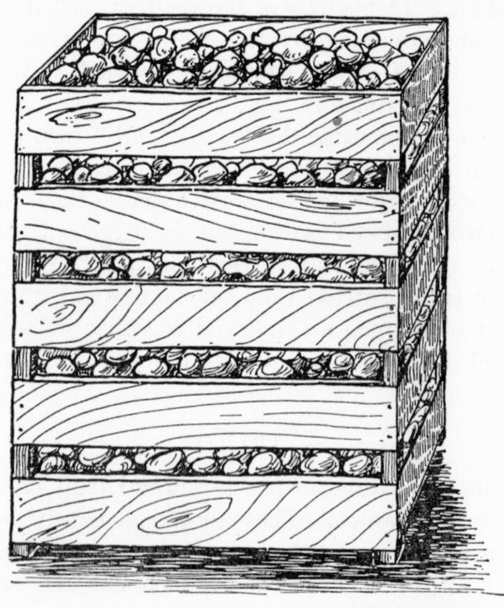

FIG. 65.—Apples and pears keep best if stored in a fruit rack. This can be constructed in sections as shown above for convenience in handling in this way, a large quantity of fruit can be stored in a small space.

is about 40 degrees Fahrenheit, and this should be aimed at by the gardener. Too much heat will result in shrivelling. Too little ventilation will cause loss through decay. By keeping an eye on stored crops, such losses can be minimised and full use made of all the produce that a well-cultivated garden can yield.

CHAPTER XV

THE USE OF SHRUBS

SHRUBS and trees are perennial plants which retain their old stems from year to year; these stems become more or less woody as they grow, and this woody texture enables them to stand up to wintry conditions when soft-stemmed plants die right back to the ground level.

There is no essential difference between a shrub and a tree, but by common consent we have grown to regard a tree as a plant that is grown on a single main stem to a considerable height, whereas a shrub sends up several stems from the ground level, and so becomes bushy at the base.

Both shrubs and trees are indispensable in garden design. One has only to note the difference between a new garden and an established one, to realise just how much we depend on trees and shrubs for backgrounds. During the past century so many delightful flowering shrubs and trees have been brought into this country that many gardens are now made using only grass and shrubs, thus saving a good deal of labour. Grass can be cut by an unskilled workman, or with a motor mower, and the actual care of shrubs means little more than a day or two spent on them every three or six months, a very different proposition from the regular care needed in herbaceous borders and formal flower-beds.

Shrubs are divided into two main groups—evergreen and deciduous or leaf-losing. Evergreens lose their leaves each season, but they do not lose the old ones until new ones have developed, so that the stems are never bare.

In both groups there are what gardeners call " flowering " and " non-flowering ". Botanically speaking many of the " non-flowering " type would be classified as flowering, the distinction being, from the gardeners' viewpoint, that some are valuable because of the brightly coloured flowers and some because of their form and foliage.

Shrubs are further divided according to the type of soil in which they prefer to grow. Many of our loveliest shrubs come from parts of America, where the soil is free of lime, and for the most part these shrubs are lime-haters or " calcifuges ", and cannot be used in gardens where the subsoil is chalky, or where surface lime dressings are given. Indeed, some plants are so temperamental in this respect that they will not thrive if watered with hard tap-water.

Still another way to classify shrubs and trees is according to their season of flowering, or in the case of foliage subjects, the season of their greatest beauty. Because there are shrubs and trees that are at their best at all the different seasons of the calendar, it is possible to make an exceedingly good and satisfactory garden with their use, and so save labour.

HOW TO CHOOSE

A few brief lists are given here, to indicate the various groups of shrubs and trees and the purpose to which they can be put in garden planning. In choosing, whether from these lists or from specialists' catalogues, these points are important:—

1. Some shrubs require more frequent pruning than others.

2. Some shrubs are specially suitable for formal designs: box, yew, privet and *Lonicera nitida* are ex-

amples of shrubs that can be clipped constantly to keep them to definite shapes.

3. Some shrubs have a loose spreading habit, some tall, perpendicular growth, some a compact outline even when unpruned. Contrasts between the habits of growth are an essential part of a beauty of a mixed shrub border, and quite as important as colour contrasts.

4. Large-leafed evergreens are heavy and sombre: their use very near the house should be limited, or they quickly become oppressive as they grow.

5. The beauty of stem and trunk should not be forgotten: silver-birch trunks set in front of cypress or yew make an attractive winter picture, so also do the red and yellow stems of willows and dogwoods.

PLANTING

Evergreens are best planted in September or in April, when the soil is warm. If possible they should be moved while quite young, and with a ball of soil kept intact round the roots, so that these do not dry out and give a severe check to the plant. Overhead watering each evening, after the tree or shrub is planted, will help it through a dry warm spell.

Evergreens can be moved when fairly large only if great care is taken to keep the soil round the roots undisturbed. A check to an evergreen, specially if it is a conifer or other tree that depends for its beauty on the unchecked development of a main stem, will ruin its symmetry, even if it does not kill the plant.

Deciduous shrubs and trees can be moved and replanted whenever the leaves are absent, but late autumn is probably the best time, as the roots have a chance to become established before the plant is called on to make a lot of new growth.

All shrub and tree planting should be done with

Fig. 66.—To plant a shrub singlehanded drive a stout stake into the hole and tie the shrub to it first, to ensure that it is at the right level.

Fig. 67.—Fill in loose soil over the roots, and tread each layer, so that all roots are in close contact with moist soil.

special care, since it is not possible to change or cultivate the subsoil after planting. Begin by opening a hole a great deal wider and deeper than seems necessary—that is to say, if you are planting a shrub with a root that extends, say, to a square foot, open out a hole at least 3 feet each way and 1 to 2 feet deep. Stand in the hole and break the bottom hard soil with a large digging fork. Toss into the hole some decaying manure or old leaves, with the roughest part of the soil that was removed, making a mound of this stony, leafy mixture in the middle of the hole. The mound should allow you to rest the shrub in position on it, with the old soil-mark on its stem coming at the original soil level of the site. If planting single-handed, drive in a stake first and tie the shrub to this before filling in any soil.

Fill the hole with the best of the soil, in which a few handfuls of bonemeal can, with advantage, be mixed. Fill in a little at a time, and tread this down over the roots, shaking the plant a little before you tread. In this way the fine soil will filter down among the roots and they will be in close contact with moist soil particles, so that they will be able to absorb food at once.

Never plant when the soil is frosty, nor when it is so wet that it is likely to cake hard over the roots.

PRUNING

General principles of pruning have already been referred to on page 125, but the gardener with some experience will need to know a little more about this subject, which is both intricate and interesting and the importance of which cannot be too highly estimated.

Shrubs naturally fall into pruning groups. There are some shrubs that develop characteristic shapes without the use of the knife—pyramid conifers, for instance. (Conifers are the cone-bearing plants—pine, cypress, spruce, etc.) There are dwarf and giant types of these, some suitable for pockets in the rock garden, and some best suited for parks and larger gardens.

There are also shrubs that do not naturally develop into symmetrical forms, but can be clipped regularly to make any desired form. Regular clipping of box, yew, and other evergreens to make them into balls, pyramids, spirals, hens and peacocks is known as **Topiary.** Clipped hedges of privet and *Lonicera nitida* are in the same group. The important thing with all these is to carry out the work very regularly, going over the plants with shears several times during spring and summer, but not too late in the autumn. If clipping is done very late in autumn, it sometimes results in brown bare patches, as new growth may have just time to develop, but not time to mature before the frosts.

Drastic pruning of foliage shrubs and trees when needed is generally done in winter. In such cases the plants must have individual treatment: where a tree has become lop-sided, for instance, it may be necessary to shorten all the branches on the one side. Care must then be taken to cut them back to a part of the branch where a side growth is developing, for if a jutting spur is left it will probably die back, and may set up disease. After all drastic pruning, the cuts made with saw or knife should be painted over, with paint, tar or creosote, to keep out rains, and so prevent the entrance of disease spores.

Finally we come to the various groups of flowering shrubs and trees. Flowering trees are as a rule left to develop their natural characters, though young standard trees may with advantage be cut back in the first year after planting, where the " head " is not already well formed. Cutting back will result in two or three radiating branches growing from each of the branches that is shortened: discretion can therefore be used, re-

PRUNING A RAMBLER

FIG. 68 (*top left*).—Rambler rose before pruning.

FIG. 69 (*top right*).—To prune a rambler cut out all the old stems right back to the ground, leaving only new stems.

FIG. 70.—Tie these to the support in several places.

PRUNING A CLIMBER

Fig. 71 (*top left*).—To prune a climbing rose (*i.e.*, a rose of similar variety to a bush rose, but with a climbing habit), first cut out weak old wood, as on a bush rose.

Fig. 72 (*top right*).—Leave a skeleton of old main stems, sufficient to cover the support.

Fig. 73.—Shorten all side growths to within an inch or two of the main stems, and tie in the main stems securely.

membering that these branches will develop immediately below each cut.

Flowering shrubs are pruned according to their habit of growth and what is required of them. If a shrub is grown for the purpose of covering a porch, archway, pillar, or pergola, pruning naturally differs from that given to the same shrub when grown as a specimen on a lawn, or in a shrub border where the size and quality of the flowers are of prime importance. It will be necessary, therefore, to modify the following brief instructions according to the position of the plants—for instance, when growing Forsythia on an archway, less severe pruning will be done than it would if the plant were one of a mixed collection of shrubs in a border.

Now let us divide shrubs according to their pruning needs, dependent on their natural habit of growth.

1. Shrubs that flower on new stems. Roses of the hybrid tea bush type such as Shot Silk, purple Buddleia, and the well-known Passion Flower, *Passiflora coerulea*, are in this class of shrubs. We prune them back early in the year, in order to limit the number of new side-growths, so that these are strong and will carry good-quality blooms. If we are pruning the rose grown as a bush, we first cut out thin, weak stems, and stems that cross the middle of the plant or rub against each other, so that they spoil its symmetry, then we cut back the remaining stems, to leave enough strong dormant buds near the base to develop into the season's new flowering wood. If, however, we are pruning a similar plant grown as a climber, we shorten the side stems only, leaving the strongest main stems to form a skeleton over the support, so that it will be well clothed in summer.

2. Shrubs that flower on one-year-old wood that developed during the previous summer. Winter Jasmine, Forsythia, and roses of the rambler type all come into this group. So do black currants. We prune these immediately they have flowered, or when the fruit has been gathered, if we want fruit. In this case all we can remove of the old wood is cut away, and only new growths left to develop, so that these new growths get the whole strength of the plant in them. Some such

FIG. 74.—Prune Forsythia after the flowers fade; cut hard back if you want good flowers another season.

shrubs will regularly send up stems from the ground level each season, and the whole of the old stems can then be removed. Some merely send out new stems from a point half-way up the old wood, and it may not be possible to remove the whole of the old stems at pruning time, but the principle is the same: as much as possible of the old wood is cut away, and new wood encouraged.

FIG. 75.—A Magnolia in early summer.

FIG. 76.—Dwarf Rhododendron, suitable shrub for a rockery pocket.

3. **Shrubs that naturally form "fruiting spurs", as in the case of orchard fruits.** Sometimes there is no need to prune at all in such cases, but often a great deal of unwanted thin wood develops, which is better thinned out, or cut back, so that the beauty of the flower is seen to greater advantage. Learn to distinguish between the dormant leaf-bud and flower-bud, and pruning will become comparatively simple.

4. **Shrubs that flower on the extreme end of the stem formed the previous season.** Lilac has this habit. Dead blooms should always be removed, but as little pruning as possible done apart from this. If, however, the plants are to be kept to a restricted size, pruning should be done immediately the flowers fade, and the method is to cut back the longest branches only, to a point where they have developed a side stem. Thus the lower side stem is left to take the place of the long stem removed, and as this stem is already half matured, it is likely to flower the following season.

5. **Shrubs that grow so slowly that pruning is unnecessary.** *Daphne mezereum* and the Japanese Quince (*Cydonia Japonica*, often called simply "Japonica") are examples.

In every case the pruner must remember that the new stems will grow immediately below the cut, and that they will develop in the direction in which the top remaining dormant buds are pointing. That is the meaning of the phrase "prune back to an outside bud"—if a dormant bud pointing out away from the centre of the shrub is the last bud left on the stem, this will develop as desired, and produce a new stem that will add to the symmetry of the plant.

In any case of doubt concerning shrub pruning, shrub specialists who supply the plants are always ready to advise, but beginners need only study the few principles outlined above, and they will soon find the way to prune correctly.

One last word—where old shrubs have overgrown their positions, it rarely does any permanent harm if they are cut back to within a foot or two of the soil in spring.

FIG. 77.—Laurustinus, or *Viburnum tinus*, the winter-flowering evergreen that will grow almost anywhere, though it grows rather slowly at first.

One or two among a large collection might die from such drastic treatment, but the majority will not only survive, but be all the better for the operation.

FOR MIXED SHRUB BORDERS

These are grouped according to the season of greatest beauty.

E. = evergreen; F. = flowering; B. = berrying or fruiting; O. = ornamental foliage or stems specially good at the stated season.

Early

Berberis aquifolium. E.F.B.
,, japonica. E.F.B.
Cornus Mas. F.
Cydonia japonica. F.
Erica mediterranea. E.F.
Daphne mezereum. F.
Forsythia. F.
Hamamelis. F.
Ribes sanguineum. F.

Late Spring and Early Summer

Ceanothus " Gloire de Versailles ". F.
Osmanthus Delavayi. E.F.
Kalmia latifolia. E.F.
Hypericum. F.
Magnolia soulangeana. F.
Philadelphus (Mock Orange). F.
Syringa (Lilacs). F.
Berberia stenophylla. E.F.
,, Darwinii. E.F.

Late Summer and Autumn

Berberis Wilsonae. O.B.
Buddleia variabilis. F.

Escallonia. E.F.
Fuchsia riccartonii. F.
Hydrangea arborescens. F.
,, paniculata. F.
Jasminum (some are semi-evergreen).
Senecio Greyii. F.O.E.
Tamarix pentandra. F.
Veronica "Autumn Glory". E.F.
,, Traversii. E.F.
Vinca major and V. minor. E.F.
Pyracantha. F.O.B.E.

Winter

Jasminum nudiflorum. F.
Chimonanthus fragrans. F.
Viburnum Tinus. E.F.
Lonicera fragrantissima. F. semi-evergreen.
Rhus cotinoides. O.
Berberis polyantha. B.
Stranvaesia. O.B.E.
Hippophae rhamnoides. O.B.

Shrubs that Need no Regular Pruning

Daphne mezereum.
Osmanthus Delavayi.
Ribes sanguineum.
Lilacs.
Ericas.
Cydonia japonica.

Shrubs that must be Pruned Immediately the Flowers Fade

Winter Jasmine.
Forsythia.
Berberis stenophylla.

Shrubs to be Pruned Back Hard in the Early Spring

Clematis of the Jackmannii group.
Buddleia variabilis.
Spiraea japonica.
Hydrangea paniculata.
Tamarix pentandra.

Note that *most* hardy shrubs need very little regular pruning, so long as they have room to develop naturally. Pruning is best restricted to thinning out crowded branches, and occasional drastic removal of older wood, where the gardener is in any doubt.

Shrubs to Use as Wall-Climbers, or on Pillars, etc.

Clematis.
Jasmine.
Honeysuckles.
Wistaria.
Ivy.
Ampelopsis (Virginian Creeper, etc.).
Roses.

(For fuller details of available shrubs see any shrub specialist's catalogue.)

GARDEN DATA

KINDS OF SOIL

Chalky.	Early and fertile if not too chalky.
Clayey.	Sticky in wet weather; hard to work. Cracks in drought. Late crops.
Hazel.	Dark brown in colour; rich.
Maiden Loam.	Top spit soil from pasture land.
Peaty.	Good for Ericas, Rhododendrons, etc.
Sandy.	Easy to work; early yields.

PATHWAY MATERIALS

BRICK.	Dutch Clinker, $4\frac{3}{4}$ in. by 3 in. by $1\frac{1}{2}$ in. Paving Brick, 9 in. by $4\frac{1}{2}$ in. by $1\frac{3}{4}$ in. Stock or Kiln, $8\frac{3}{4}$ in. by $4\frac{1}{4}$ in. by $2\frac{3}{4}$ in. A load of bricks equals 500. 1 sq. yd. of paving requires 32 bricks laid flat, 48 bricks laid on edge. Some bricks will not stand frosts.
GRASS.	Edging of stone or tile makes cutting easy.
GRAVEL.	Dress with bitumin to prevent weeds, looseness, and lifting by frost.
STEPPING STONES.	Ripple-faced sandstone. 1 ton covers approximately 8 sq. yds. Allow a short space between stones.

MATERIALS FOR CRAZY-PAVING

Limestone.	Ripple-faced, light coloured. No cement.
Somerset.	Rough-faced, brown, 2 in. thick. Use 8–10 yds. to the ton. Smooth-faced, light grey, 1–$1\frac{1}{2}$ in. thick. 10–12 sq. yds. to the ton.
Sandstone.	Similar to York, $1\frac{1}{2}$ in. thick. 1 ton covers 10 sq. yds. Red, $1\frac{1}{2}$ in. thick.
Welsh.	Dark grey stone, $1\frac{1}{2}$ in. thick.

SQUARE PAVING MATERIALS. Quarry trimmed.

Welsh.	As above.
York.	Light brown, self-faced. 1 ton covers 10–11 sq. yds. Non-flaking and frost proof.
	Many crazy-paving stones are quarry trimmed for random work.
Sandstone.	Light brown, hard. Used for "dry" wall, 2 to 4 in. thick.
York.	Greyish-brown. Used for formal cemented walls. 1 ton builds approx. 4 super yds. of wall.

RETAINING WALLS

Thickness approx. one-third the vertical height. One weephole required to every superficial yard of wall. Tilt wall backwards of not less than 1½ in. in 1 ft.

FLOWER-POTS: Sizes

The following table gives the names and the equivalent sizes :—

Names.	Diameter, ins.
Thimbles	2
Thumbs	2½
60's	3
48's	4½
32's	6
24's	8½
16's	9
12's	11½
8's	12
6's	13
4's	15
2's	18

Gardeners frequently refer to flower-pots by special names—*e.g.*, "thumbs," 48's, etc.

INDEX

GIVE INSTRUCTION TO A WISE MAN . . .